# God's
# BIG
# HANDBOOK
# FOR THE SOUL

*An Owner's Manual*

# God's
# BIG
# HANDBOOK
# FOR THE SOUL

*An Owner's Manual*

COMPILED BY JULIET MABEY

ONEWORLD
OXFORD

GOD'S BIG HANDBOOK FOR THE SOUL

Oneworld Publications
(Sales and Editorial)
185 Banbury Road
Oxford OX2 7AR
England
http://www.oneworld-publications.com

Oneworld Publications
(US Office)
160 N Washington St.
4th floor, Boston
MA 02114

ISBN 1–85168–187–6

*Cover and text design by* Design Deluxe, Bath
*Printed by* Graphicom Srl, Vicenza, Italy

# CONTENTS

# PREFACE

ANY OF us today feel a deep-seated need to find greater value and meaning in our lives. No matter how much money we have, or how large a car or house, or how successful a career, without an understanding of who we are and of our place in the "bigger" scheme of things, our lives can feel shallow and empty. This vague feeling of alienation is a symptom of a spiritual crisis. In the hurly-burly of modern life, we sometimes neglect that most essential part of ourselves – our soul.

St. Ignatius Loyola defined the essential nature of a human being in his famous statement: "I come from God, I belong to God, I am destined for God!" Plotinus speaks of the human soul as indivisible from the All Soul – a piece of the divine within us all. Our soul is our essential inner reality, capable of reflecting all the divine qualities, and being of God, it is destined to return to God. To find fulfillment, we must have a sense of purpose in life, we must understand who we are, what our potential is, and how we can achieve it. From this perspective, our purpose in this physical world is to direct our souls God-ward, so that our lives will be spiritually enriched and meaningful.

Just as our bodies need food and warmth, sleep and exercise, so our souls need careful attention if they are to thrive and develop to their full potential. Our soul represents the unique essence of who we are: it is in the soul that our capacity to experience true happiness and meaning in life lies, and it is through the soul that we connect to others, to the world around us, and to God. Getting to know and care for our soul, however, requires conscious effort. John Keats called this world the "vale of soul-making" – life here on earth is our laboratory. Fostering the development of our soul requires the spiritual discipline to turn our hearts toward God and to spiritualize our thoughts and actions, not by living apart from the real world, but by engaging fully in it, living the everyday within the consciousness of the eternal.

How can we nurture our souls in our daily lives? This little anthology offers a wealth of inspiration drawn from the religions and philosophies of the past as well as from the words of well-known writers and prominent people of modern times. Here they share their insights as to how we may all enhance our connections with a higher source, exploring who we are, our ultimate goal in life, how to develop a personal relationship with God, and how this might be translated into a daily program for a healthy soul. Together they offer us a handbook to help us along the spiritual path.

JULIET MABEY

# THE WORLD OF THE SOUL

*The things that are seen are temporal; the things that are unseen are eternal.*

RALPH WALDO EMERSON, *Nature*

# THE UNIQUENESS
## OF A HUMAN BEING

O<sup>UR SOUL</sup> is made to be God's dwelling-place; and the dwelling-place of the soul is God, which is unmade.

JULIAN OF NORWICH, *Revelations of Divine Love*

I AM THE nucleus of every creature, Arjuna; for without me nothing can exist, neither animate nor inanimate . . . Wherever you find strength, or beauty, or spiritual power, you may be sure that these have sprung from a spark of my essence.

HINDUISM: Bhagavad Gita 10.39–41

T HE SOUL is in God and God in the soul, just as the fish is in the sea and the sea in the fish.

ST. CATHERINE OF SIENA

M AN – the true man – is soul, not body; though physically man belongs to the animal kingdom, yet his soul lifts him above the rest of creation. Behold how the light of the sun illuminates the world of matter: even so doth the Divine Light shed its rays in the kingdom of the soul. The soul it is which makes the human creature a celestial entity!

BAHÁ'Í FAITH: Paris Talks 85

NO ONE can give a definition of the soul. But we know what it feels like. The soul is the sense of something higher than ourselves, something that stirs in us thoughts, hopes, and aspirations which go out to the world of goodness, truth, and beauty. The soul is a burning desire to breathe in this world of light and never to lose it – to remain children of light.

ALBERT SCHWEITZER

THE SOUL of man is immortal and imperishable.

PLATO, *Dialogues*

THESE BODIES are perishable; but the dwellers in these bodies are eternal, indestructible, and impenetrable.

HINDUISM: *Bhagavad Gita 2.18*

W HEN JUDAISM speaks of immortality . . . its primary meaning is that man contains something independent of the flesh and surviving it: his consciousness and moral capacity; his essential personality; a soul.

MILTON STEINBERG, *Basic Judaism*

D ESPISE THE flesh, for it passes away; be solicitous for your soul, which will never die.

ST. BASIL

O UR SPIRIT is a being of a nature quite indestructible and its activity continues from eternity to eternity. It is like the sun, which seems to set only to our earthly eyes, but which, in reality, never sets, but shines on unceasingly.

J.W. VON GOETHE, *Conversations with Eckermann, I*

THE HUMAN spirit is hidden, unknowable. Through our words and actions we reveal the inner nature of its spiritual substance. The essence of this spirit is unchanging, but its expression – our words and actions – is fleeting and subject to change. Our prayer, spiritual battles, and fasting are all transient, but the spirit that gave rise to them remains for ever. Our human spirit rubbed its substance on the touchstone of divine command.

RUMI, *Masnavi V.246–50*

EACH OF us possesses a soul, but we do not prize our souls as creatures made in God's image deserve, and so we do not understand the great secrets which they contain.

ST. TERESA OF ÁVILA, *The Interior Castle*

THE SOUL, mindful of its ethereal nature, presses upward with exceedingly great force, and struggles with its weight. It distrusts things seen . . . It seeks those things which truly and everlastingly are.

DESIDERIUS ERASMUS, Enchiridion

THE SOUL is a sign of God, a heavenly gem whose reality the most learned of men hath failed to grasp, and whose mystery no mind, however acute, can ever hope to unravel. It is the first among all created things to declare the excellence of its Creator, the first to recognize His glory, to cleave to His truth, and to bow down in adoration before Him. If it be faithful to God, it will reflect His light, and will, eventually, return unto Him. If it fails, however, in its allegiance to its Creator, it will become a victim to self and passion, and will, in the end, sink in their depths.

BAHÁ'Í FAITH: Gleanings 158

IN ITS highest sense [the soul is] a vast capacity for God . . . A chamber with elastic and contractile walls, which can be expanded, with God as its guest, illimitably, but which without God shrinks and shrinks until every vestige of the divine is gone, and God's image is kept without God's Spirit.

HENRY DRUMMOND, *Natural Law in the Spiritual World*

I CAN FIND nothing with which to compare the great beauty of a soul and its great capacity. The very fact that his majesty says it is made in his image means that we can hardly form any conception of the soul's great dignity and beauty.

ST. TERESA OF ÁVILA

T HE SOUL is characterized by knowledge and vision, is formless, an agent, has the same extent as its own body, is the enjoyer of the fruits of karmas, and exists in samsara. It is also enlightened and has a characteristic upward motion.

JAINISM: *Nemichandra, Dravyasangraha 2*


I BELIEVE IN the absolute oneness of God and therefore of humanity. What though we have many bodies? We have but one soul . . . I know God is neither in heaven nor down below, but in everyone.

MOHANDAS K. GANDHI

# UNDERSTANDING YOUR
# INNER REALITY

S PIRIT IS the only reality. It is the inner being of the world,
that which essentially is, and is *per se*.

G.W.F. HEGEL, *Phenomenology of Mind*

THE KINGDOM of God is not coming with signs to be observed, nor will they say, "Lo, here it is!" or "There!" for behold, the kingdom of God is within you.

CHRISTIANITY: *Luke 17.20–1*

HE, THE eternal, dwells concealed in the heart of all beings. Though himself devoid of all senses, he is the illuminator of all the senses, the source of their powers.

HINDUISM: *Mahanirvana Tantra*

MAN IS made for the contemplation of heaven, and is in truth a heavenly plant, to come to the knowledge of God.

ST. CLEMENT OF ALEXANDRIA, *Exhortation to the Greeks*

THOUGH OUR natural life were no life, but rather a continual dying, yet we have two lives besides that, an eternal life reserved for heaven, but yet a heavenly life too, a spiritual life, even in this world.

JOHN DONNE, *sermon*

IN MAN there are two natures; his spiritual or higher nature and his material or lower nature. In one he approaches God, in the other he lives for the world alone. Signs of both these natures are to be found in men.

BAHÁ'Í FAITH: *Paris Talks 60*

STRIVE EARNESTLY and be assured that only this body of yours, and not your real self, is mortal. For you are not the mere physical form that you appear to be; but the real man is the soul and not that physical body which men can point to. Know, then, that your true nature is divine, if indeed it is a divine principle which lives, feels, remembers, and foresees, and which rules, guides, and activates the body beneath its sway, even as the supreme God directs the universe. And as the world, which is in part mortal, is stirred to motion by God himself, who lives forever, so the frail body is quickened by an immortal soul.

CICERO, *On the Commonwealth*

I F ONE is out of touch with the purpose of something, one is out of touch with the reality of that thing. Suppose, for example, that someone wins a refrigerator in a contest and, not understanding the purpose of the refrigerator, stores his boots in it and puts it on the front porch to display to the neighbors. A person who relates to a refrigerator by using it as a closet for his boots is out of touch with the reality of that refrigerator because he does not understand its purpose. Not to understand the purpose of the refrigerator means that one is not able to make use of its essential power – refrigeration.

What happens then if a human being is out of touch with his reality because he does not understand his purpose? He becomes self-alienated. One who is self-alienated does not know who he is or where he is going.

The primary way through which we come in contact with the reality of things is to understand their purpose. Therefore if we want to be in touch with our own reality and have the maximum amount of meaning in this life, we must gain a clearer apprehension of our purpose . . . our purpose is to know and to love God. Our reality is to express that knowledge and love by reflecting or mirroring forth the attributes of God, a capacity that we have been given. It is a critical part of comprehending God's purpose for man for us to know what these attributes are and what we have to do in order to develop them.

DANIEL JORDAN, *Becoming Your True Self*

W E ONLY see the outer covering of reality and it's only when our inner senses are opened, when our inner life is opened, that we pierce through the unreality.

SISTER PASCALINE COFF

THERE IS no reality except the one contained within us. This is why so many people lead such an unreal life. They take the images outside them for reality and never allow the world within to assert itself.

HERMAN HESSE

THE MAN who has no inner life is the slave of his surroundings.

HENRI FREDERIC AMIEL

THE GREAT malady of the twentieth century, implicated in all of our troubles and affecting us individually and socially, is "loss of the soul." When soul is neglected, it doesn't just go away; it appears symptomatically in obsessions, addictions, violence, and loss of meaning. Our temptation is to isolate these symptoms or to try to eradicate them one by one; but the root problem is that we have lost our wisdom about the soul, even our interest in it.

THOMAS MOORE, *Care of the Soul*

Human beings need spiritual as well as material sustenance. Without spiritual sustenance, it is difficult to get and maintain peace of mind.

The Dalai Lama

Without an awareness of what we are, the unique pattern of God within each individual won't be expressed. Every human being, like every flower, has a unique pattern of expression. We all have a kaleidoscope of good in us – a deeper dimension accessed through our awareness that God is expressed through us and as us. So, it's not only important, it's the only game in town. It's the reason we're here.

A rose's purpose is to grow and become strong enough to bloom. When you have matured spiritually, you bloom into an awareness of your oneness with God. Without that awareness, you are immature, regardless of how much you have attained in the world materialistically, intellectually, or emotionally.

Rev. Michael Beckwith, *What Personal Life?*

THE SOUL says to her base earthly parts, "My
    exile is more bitter than yours: I am
    celestial."
The body desires green herbs and running
    water, because its origin is from those;
The soul desires life and the Living One,
    because its origin is the Infinite Soul.
The desire of the soul is for knowledge and
    wisdom; the desire of the body is for
    orchards, meadows, and vines.
The desire of the soul is for ascent and
    sublimity; the desire of the body is for gain
    and the means of self-indulgence.

RUMI, *Masnavi III.4435–9*

# THE DESTINY OF THE SOUL

A RELIGIOUS MAN is guided in his activity not by the consequences of his action, but by the consciousness of the destination of his life.

LEO TOLSTOY, *Confessions*

THE DESTINY of man is not limited to his existence on earth and he must never forget that fact.

PIERRE LECOMTE DU NOÜY, *Human Destiny*

WE ARE not made to rest in this world. It is not our true native land.

FATHER ANDREW, *In the Silence*

IF HEAVEN is our country, what is the earth but a place of exile? If the departure out of the world is but an entrance into life, what is the world but a sepulcher? What is a continuance in it but an absorption in death?

JOHN CALVIN, *Institutes III*

T HE BODY of a man is not a home but an inn – and that only briefly.

SENECA, *Letters to Lucilius*

T HOSE WHO hope for no other life are dead even for this.

J.W. VON GOETHE

T HINK OF yourself as a seed patiently wintering in the earth; waiting to come up a flower in the gardener's good time, up into the real world, the real waking.

C.S. LEWIS

WE CALL this life, that is life's preparation;
We call this life, a little time of tears;
But think you God for this designed creation,
A few short years?

DOUGLAS MALLOCH, *We Call This Life*

I N THIS world [man] must prepare himself for the life beyond. That which he needs in the world of the Kingdom must be obtained here. Just as he prepared himself in the world of the matrix by acquiring forces necessary in this sphere of existence, so, likewise, the indispensable forces of the divine existence must be potentially attained in this world.

What is he in need of in the Kingdom which transcends the life and limitation of this mortal sphere? That world beyond is a world of sanctity and radiance; therefore, it is necessary that in this world he should acquire these divine attributes. In that world there is need of spirituality, faith, assurance, the knowledge and love of God. These he must attain in this world so that after his ascension from the earthly to the heavenly Kingdom he shall find all that is needful in that eternal life ready for him.

That divine world is manifestly a world of lights; therefore, man has need of illumination here. That is a world of love; the love of God is essential. It is a world of perfections; virtues, or perfections, must be acquired. That world is vivified by the breaths of the Holy Spirit; in this world we must seek them. That is the Kingdom of everlasting life; it must be attained during this vanishing existence.

By what means can man acquire these things? How shall he obtain these merciful gifts and powers? First, through the knowledge of God. Second, through the love of God. Third, through faith. Fourth, through philanthropic deeds. Fifth, through self-sacrifice. Sixth, through severance from this world. Seventh, through sanctity and holiness.

BAHÁ'Í FAITH: *Promulgation of Universal Peace 225–6*

GLORIOUS GOD, give me grace to amend my life, and to have an eye to my end without begrudging death, which to those who die in you, good Lord, is the gate of a wealthy life.

SIR THOMAS MORE

THIS WORLD is like a vestibule before the world to come; prepare yourself in the vestibule that you may enter the hall.

JUDAISM: *Mishnah, Abot 4.21*

O PEOPLE! FEAR God, and whatever you do, do it anticipating death. Try to attain everlasting blessing in return for transitory and perishable wealth, power, and pleasures of this world.

Be prepared for a fast passage because here you are destined for a short stay. Always be ready for death, for you are living under its shadow. Be wise like people who have heard the message of God and have taken a warning from it . . .

You must remember to gather from this life such harvest as will be of use and help to you hereafter.

ISLAM: *Nahjul Balagha, Sermon 67*

O SHREWD businessman, do only profitable business: deal only in that commodity which shall accompany you after death.

SIKHISM: *Adi Granth, Sri Raga M.1*

THOSE FOR whom the belief in immortality is most vivid are the most likely to practice the virtues which have a survival value and the least likely to deviate into either those virtues or those vices which are exclusively human.

JOSEPH WOOD KRUTCH, *The Modern Temper*

I OFTEN FEEL that death is not the enemy of life, but its friend, for it is the knowledge that our years are limited which makes them so precious. It is the truth that time is but lent to us which makes us, at our best, look upon our years as a trust handed into our temporary keeping.

JOSHUA LOTH LIEBMAN

THE SOUL that hath remained faithful to the Cause of God, and stood unwaveringly firm in His Path shall, after his ascension, be possessed of such power that all the worlds which the Almighty hath created can benefit through him. Such a soul provideth, at the bidding of the Ideal King and Divine Educator, the pure leaven that leaveneth the world of being, and furnisheth the power through which the arts and wonders of the world are made manifest. Consider how meal needeth leaven to be leavened with. Those souls that are the symbols of detachment are the leaven of the world.

BAHÁ'Í FAITH: *Gleanings 160–1*

EW CROSS the river of time and reach Nirvana. Most of them run up and down on this side of the river.

But those who, when they know the law, follow the path of the law, shall reach the other shore and go beyond the realm of death.

BUDDHISM: *Dhammapada 85–6*

# IN SEARCH OF MEANING

M AN WAS meant to realize the divine potential within him. He misses the mark when he fails to do so. He has attained salvation when he achieves his full spiritual potential as a human being, created in the image of God.

ROLAND B. GITTELSOHN, *The Meaning of Judaism*

SALVATION IS not putting a man into heaven, but putting heaven into man.

MALTBIE D. BABCOCK, *Thoughts for Everyday Living*

THE ROOT-WORD *buddh* means to wake up, to know, to understand; and he or she who wakes up and understands is called a Buddha. It is as simple as that. The capacity to wake up, to understand, and to love is called Buddha nature. When Buddhists say "I take refuge in the Buddha," they are expressing trust in their own capacity of understanding, of becoming awake. The Chinese and the Vietnamese say, "I go back and rely on the Buddha in me." Adding "in me" makes it very clear that you yourself are the Buddha.

THICH NHAT HANH, *Being Peace*

THE PURPOSE of God in creating man hath been, and will ever be, to enable him to know his Creator and attain His Presence.

BAHÁ'Í FAITH: *Gleanings 29*

OUR WORDS and actions testify to our hidden thoughts; together they express our inner spirit. This is our life's testimony, our purpose here on earth: to manifest the very nature of our spirit, which is touched by the spirit of God.

RUMI, *Masnavi V.236, 250*

IF GRAINS of sand can become a reflection of the divine, just think what can happen to the human being.

THE DALAI LAMA

I THINK OF our whole life, from the time we're born, as a spiritual journey in search of the experience of oneness with the divine.

RIANE EISLER, *The Long Journey Home*

THE WORLD with all its goods cannot content the heart of man; for he was created not for them, but for God alone; hence God alone can make him happy and content.

ST. ALPHONSUS DE LIGUORI, *Preface for Death*

SINCE, O my soul, thou art capable of God, woe to thee if thou contentest thyself with anything less than God.

ST. FRANCIS DE SALES

THE ROSE window high above seems black and formless. But when we enter, and see it backlit by the sun, it dazzles in astonishing splendor. And it reminds us that without faith, we too are but stained-glass windows in the dark.

GEORGE BUSH

AND A soul and Him who perfected it
And inspired it with conscience of what is
    wrong and right.
He is indeed successful who purifies his soul,
And he is indeed a failure who corrupts it.

ISLAM: *Qur'an 41.7–10*

ULTIMATELY FAITH is the only key to the universe. The final meaning of human existence, and the answers to the questions on which all our happiness depends, cannot be found in any other way.

THOMAS MERTON

IF THERE is God and there is a future life, then there is truth and there is goodness; and the highest happiness of man consists in striving for their attainment.

LEO TOLSTOY, *War and Peace*

LET US see to it . . . that our lives, like jewels of great price, be noteworthy not because of their width, but because of their weight. Let us measure them by their performance, not their duration.

SENECA

GOD HAS placed a ladder before our feet: we
    must climb it, step by step.
You have feet: why pretend to be lame? You have
    hands: why conceal the fingers that grip? . . .
If you bear God's burden, He will raise you up.
If you accept His commands, He will shower
    you with His grace and bounty.
If you seek union with Him, you will become
    united for evermore.

RUMI, *Masnavi I.929–31, 936–7*

# A PSALM OF LIFE

TELL ME not, in mournful numbers
Life is but an empty dream!
For the soul is dead that slumbers,
And things are not what they seem.

Life is real! Life is earnest!
And the grave is not its goal;
Dust thou art, to dust returnest,
Was not spoken of the soul.

Not enjoyment, and not sorrow,
Is our destined end or way;
But to act, that each tomorrow
Find us farther than today.

Art is long, and time is fleeting,
And our hearts, though stout and brave,
Still, like muffled drums, are beating
Funeral marches to the grave.

In the world's broad field of battle,
In the bivouac of life,
Be not like dumb, driven cattle!
Be a hero in the strife!

Trust no future, howe'er pleasant!
Let the dead past bury its dead!
Act – act in the living present!
Heart within, and God o'erhead!

Lives of great men all remind us
We can make our lives sublime,
And, departing, leave behind us
Footprints on the sands of time;

Footprints, that perhaps another,
Sailing o'er life's solemn main,
A forlorn and shipwrecked brother,
Seeing, shall take heart again.

Let us, then, be up and doing,
With a heart for any fate;
Still achieving, still pursuing,
Learn to labor and to wait.

HENRY WADSWORTH LONGFELLOW

YOU ARE here in order to enable the world to live more amply, with greater vision, with a finer spirit of hope and achievement. You are here to enrich the world, and you impoverish yourself if you forget the errand.

WOODROW WILSON

THE AIM, if reached or not, makes great the life. Try to be Shakespeare, leave the rest to fate.

ROBERT BROWNING

IT MATTERS not whether a man does much or little, if only he directs his heart toward heaven.

JUDAISM: *Talmud*

# THE SOUL'S QUEST

*Behold! A sacred voice is calling you! All over the sky a sacred voice is calling you!*

NATIVE AMERICAN TRADITION: *Black Elk*

# FINDING YOUR TRUE NORTH

IF I LOSE my direction I have to look for the
   North Star, and I go to the north.
That does not mean I expect to arrive at the
   North Star;
I just want to go in that direction.

THICH NHAT HANH

GOD HAS planted in your heart the desire to search for Him. Do not look at your weaknesses but focus on the search. Every seeker is worthy of this search. Strive to redouble your efforts, so that your soul may escape from this material prison.

RUMI: *Masnavi V.1733–5*

NONE BUT God can satisfy the longings of an immortal soul; that as the heart was made for him, so he only can fill it.

RICHARD CHENEVIX TRENCH,
*Notes on the Parables: The Prodigal Son*

THE INFINITE goodness has such wide arms that it takes whatever turns to it.

DANTE, *The Divine Comedy*

MAN IS confronted by something spiritually greater than himself which, in contrast to human nature and to all other phenomena, is absolute reality. And this absolute reality of which man is aware is also an absolute good for which he is athirst.

A.J. TOYNBEE, *An Historian's Approach to Religion*

LATE HAVE I loved Thee, O Beauty so ancient and so new; late have I loved Thee: for behold Thou wert within me, and I outside; and I sought Thee outside and in my unloveliness fell upon those lovely things that Thou hast made. Thou wert with me, and I was not with Thee. I was kept from Thee by those things, yet had they not been in Thee, they would not have been at all. Thou didst call and cry to me to break open my deafness; and Thou didst send forth Thy beams and shine upon me and chase away my blindness. Thou didst breathe fragrance upon me, and I drew in my breath and do now pant for Thee. I tasted Thee, and now hunger and thirst for Thee. Thou didst touch me, and I have burned for Thy peace.

ST. AUGUSTINE

YOU WILL seek me and find me when you seek me with all your heart.

JUDAISM: *Jeremiah 29*

NO MAN that seeketh Us will We ever disappoint, neither shall he that hath set his face toward Us be denied access unto Our court.

BAHÁ'Í FAITH: *Gleanings 126*

THE WINDS of God's grace are always blowing; it is for us to raise our sails.

HINDUISM: *Ascribed to Ramakrishna*

HOW IS it, then, that the voice of God is not more distinctly heard by men? The answer to this question is: to be heard it must be listened for.

DÉSIRÉ JOSEPH MERCIER, *Conferences*

HERE IN the maddening maze of things,
When tossed by storm or flood,
To one fixed ground my spirit clings,
I know that God is good.

I know not what the future hath,
Of marvel or surprise,
Assured alone that life and death,
His mercy underlies.

I know not where his islands lift,
Their fronded palms in air,
I only know I cannot drift,
Beyond his love and care.

JOHN GREENLEAF WHITTIER

A LOVER never seeks without being sought by his
  beloved.
When the lightning bolt of love has pierced this
  heart, be assured that there is love in that
  heart.
When the love of God grows in your heart,
  beyond any doubt God loves you.

RUMI, *Masnavi III. 4393–6*

MIGHT I behold thee,
Might I know thee,
Might I consider thee,
Might I understand thee,
O Lord of the universe.

NATIVE AMERICAN TRADITION: *Inca Song*

The world and that infinite variety of pleasing objects in it, do so allure and enamor us, that we cannot so much as look toward God, seek him, or think on him as we should.

ROBERT BURTON, *The Anatomy of Melancholy III*

ULTIMATE REALITY is not clearly and immediately apprehended except by those who have made themselves loving, pure in heart, and poor in spirit.

ALDOUS HUXLEY, *The Perennial Philosophy*

GOD DOES not die on the day when we cease to believe in a personal deity, but we die on the day when our lives cease to be illumined by the steady radiance, renewed daily, of a wonder, the source of which is beyond all reason.

DAG HAMMARSKJÖLD, *Markings*

AS ONE can ascend to the top of a house by means of a ladder or a bamboo or a staircase or a rope, so divers are the ways and means to approach God, and every religion in the world shows one of these ways.

SRI RAMAKRISHNA, *His Life and Sayings*

LIKE THE bee gathering honey from different flowers, the wise man accepts the essence of different scriptures and sees only the good in all religions.

HINDUISM: *Srimad Bhagavatam*

GOD HAS given man the eye of investigation by which he may see and recognize truth. He has endowed man with ears that he may hear the message of reality and conferred upon him the gift of reason by which he may discover things for himself. This is his endowment and equipment for the investigation of reality. Man is not intended to see through the eyes of another, hear through another's ears, or comprehend with another's brain.

BAHÁ'Í FAITH: *Promulgation of Universal Peace 293*

GO GODWARD: thou wilt find a road.

RUSSIAN PROVERB

# SEEKING NEARNESS TO GOD

Y OU HAVE made us for yourself and our hearts are restless until they rest in you.

ST. AUGUSTINE OF HIPPO, *Confessions*

LOVE MEANS that the attributes of the lover are changed into those of the Beloved.

JUNAYD OF BAGDAD, *Al Marghināni, al-Hidāya*

LOVE UNITES the soul with God: and the more love the soul has, the more powerfully it enters into God and is centered on him.

ST. JOHN OF THE CROSS, *The Living Flame of Love*

WHAT IS the fitting love of God? It should be as if he were lovesick, unable to get the woman he loves out of his mind, pining for her constantly when he is at rest and in motion, when he eats and drinks. Even more than this should be the love of God in the heart of those who love him and yearn constantly for him, as he commanded us: "With all your heart and with all your soul."

MOSES MAIMONIDES

B E AWARE of me always, adore me, make every act an offering to me, and you shall come to me; this I promise, for you are dear to me.

HINDUISM: *Bhagavad Gita 18.65*

G OD HAS declared: I am close to the thought that My servant has of Me, and I am with him whenever he recollects Me. If he remembers Me in himself, I remember him in Myself, and if he remembers Me in a gathering I remember him better than those in the gathering do, and if he approaches Me by as much as one hand's length, I approach him by a cubit . . . If he takes a step toward Me, I run toward him.

ISLAM: *Hadith*

B EHOLD, I stand at the door and knock; if anyone hears my voice and opens the door, I will come in to him and eat with him, and he with me.

CHRISTIANITY: *Revelation 3.20*

NO SEPARATION exists between the Beloved and
the lover.
I do not belong to myself. I am His possession.

RÁBI'A

WHEN YOU die to yourself and come alive through
God, in truth you have become one with God,
in absolute unity.

RUMI, *Masnavi IV.2766–7*

IT IS only by forgetting yourself that you draw near to God.

HENRY DAVID THOREAU

A HUMBLE KNOWLEDGE of thyself is a surer way to God than a deep search after learning.

THOMAS À KEMPIS, *The Imitation of Christ*

MAY ALL I say and all I think
Be in harmony with thee,
God within me,
God beyond me,
Maker of the trees.

NATIVE AMERICAN TRADITION: *Chinook*

IN THY image let me pattern my life, O Ahura
   Mazda,
Let me awake with thy name on my lips
In my eyes let me ever carry thy image
To enable me to perceive thee,
And thee alone, in everyone else.

ZOROASTRIANISM

GOD BE in my head
   and in my understanding;
God be in my eyes
   and in my looking;
God be in my mouth
   and in my speaking;
God be in my heart
   and in my thinking;
God be at my end
   and at my departing.

CHRISTIANITY: Book of Hours

O THOU
Who hast given me eyes
To see the light
That fills my room,
Give me the inward vision
To behold thee in this place.

O thou
Who hast made me to feel
The morning wind upon my limbs,
Help me to feel thy presence
As I bow in worship of thee.

CHANDRA DEVANESEN

NEARNESS TO God cannot be calculated. To be near to God is not to go up or down, but to escape from the prison of existence. The treasure of God lies in non-existence. You are deluded by existence. How could you understand what non-existence is?

RUMI, *Masnavi III.4513–16*

THE GREATEST attainment in the world of humanity is nearness to God. Every lasting glory, honor, grace, and beauty which comes to man comes through nearness to God. All the Prophets and apostles longed and prayed for nearness to the Creator . . . Nearness to God is possible through devotion to Him, through entrance into the Kingdom and service to humanity; it is attained by unity with mankind and through loving-kindness to all; it is dependent upon investigation of truth, acquisition of praiseworthy virtues, service in the cause of universal peace and personal sanctification. In a word, nearness to God necessitates sacrifice of self, severance, and the giving up of all to Him. Nearness is likeness.

BAHÁ'Í FAITH: *Promulgation of Universal Peace 147–8*

I WILL TRY to find a lift by which I may be raised to God, for I am too small to climb the steep stairway to perfection.

St. Thérèse of Lisieux

# A SPIRITUAL LIFE

A SPIRITUAL LIFE is simply a life in which all that we do comes from the center, where we are anchored in God.

EVELYN UNDERHILL, *The Spiritual Life*

TRUE RELIGION is real living; living with all one's soul, with all one's goodness and righteousness.

ALBERT EINSTEIN

WHEREIN DOES religion consist? It consists in doing as little harm as possible, in doing good in abundance, in the practice of love, of compassion, of truthfulness, and purity in all the walks of life.

ASOKA, *Edicts*

THE WAY of heaven has no favorites. It is always with the good man.

TAOISM: *The Way of Lao-Tze*

LET NO one deceive another,
Let no one despise another in any situation,
Let no one, from antipathy or hatred, wish evil
to anyone.
Just as a mother, with her own life, protects her
only son from hurt,
So within yourself foster a limitless concern for
every living creature.
Display a heart of boundless love for all the
world
In all its height and depth and broad extent,
Love unrestrained, without hate or enmity.
Then as you stand or walk, sit or lie, until
overcome by drowsiness,
Devote your mind entirely to this; it is known as
living here life divine.

BUDDHISM

A NYONE CAN carry his burden, however hard, until nightfall. Anyone can do his work, however hard, for one day. Anyone can live sweetly, patiently, lovingly, purely, till the sun goes down. And this is all that life really means.

ROBERT LOUIS STEVENSON

DO ALL the good you can
By all the means you can
In all the ways you can
In all the places you can
To all the people you can
As long as ever you can.

JOHN WESLEY, *Role*

TREAT PEOPLE in such a way and live amongst them in such a manner that if you die they will weep over you; alive they crave for your company.

ISLAM: *Nahjul Balagha, Saying 9*

IF I can stop one heart from breaking,
I shall not live in vain:
If I can ease one life the aching,
Or cool one pain,
Or help one fainting robin
Unto his nest again,
I shall not live in vain.

EMILY DICKINSON

THE TRUE believers are those whose hearts are filled with awe at the mention of God, and whose faith grows stronger as they listen to His revelations. They put their trust in their Lord, pray steadfastly, and give in alms of that which We have given them.

Such are the true believers. They shall be exalted and forgiven by their Lord, and a generous provision shall be made for them.

ISLAM: *Qur'an 8.2–4*

IF YOU can keep your head when all about you
    Are losing theirs and blaming it on you;
If you can trust yourself when all men doubt you,
    But make allowance for their doubting too;
If you can wait and not be tired by waiting,
    Or, being lied about, don't deal in lies,
Or, being hated, don't give way to hating,
    And yet don't look too good, nor talk too wise;

If you can dream – and not make dreams your master;
    If you can think – and not make thoughts your aim;
If you can meet with triumph and disaster
    And treat those two impostors just the same;
If you can bear to hear the truth you've spoken
    Twisted by knaves to make a trap for fools,
Or watch the things you gave your life to broken,
    And stoop and build 'em up with worn-out tools;

If you can make one heap of all your winnings
    And risk it on one turn of pitch-and-toss,
And lose, and start again at your beginnings
    And never breathe a word about your loss;
If you can force your heart and nerve and sinew
    To serve your turn long after they are gone,
And so hold on when there is nothing in you
    Except the will which says to them: "Hold on!"

If you can talk with crowds and keep your virtue,
    Or walk with kings – nor lose the common touch;
If neither foes nor loving friends can hurt you;
    If all men count with you, but none too much;
If you can fill the unforgiving minute
    With sixty seconds' worth of distance run –
Yours is the earth and everything that's in it,
    And – which is more – you'll be a man, my son!

RUDYARD KIPLING

T O REFRAIN from evil, to cultivate good, to purify one's mind – this is the teaching of the Buddhas.

BUDDHISM: *Dhammapada 183*

A ND HOW, you ask, are we to walk the spiritual path? We answer: say little, and love much; give all; judge no man; aspire to all that is pure and good.

NATIVE AMERICAN TRADITION: *White Eagle*

D O NO wrong nor hate your neighbor; for it is not he that you wrong; you wrong yourself.

NATIVE AMERICAN TRADITION: *Shawnee Chant*

O YE LOVERS of God! Be kind to all peoples; care for every person; do all ye can to purify the hearts and minds of men; strive ye to gladden every soul. To every meadow be a shower of grace, to every tree the water of life; be as sweet musk to the sense of humankind, and to the ailing be a fresh, restoring breeze. Be pleasing waters to all those who thirst, a careful guide to all who have lost their way; be father and mother to the orphans; be loving sons and daughters to the old; be an abundant treasure to the poor. Think ye of love and good fellowship as the delights of heaven; think ye of hostility and hatred as the torments of hell.

BAHÁ'Í FAITH: *Selections from the Writings of 'Abdu'l-Bahá 245*

O MAY I join the choir invisible
Of those immortal dead who live again
In minds made better by their presence; live
In pulses stirred to generosity,
In deeds of daring rectitude, in scorn
Of miserable aims that end with self,
In thoughts sublime that pierce the night like stars,
And with their mild persistence urge men's minds
To vaster issues . . .
                    May I reach
That purest heaven – be to other souls
The cup of strength in some great agony,
Enkindle generous ardor, feed pure love,
Beget the smiles that have no cruelty,
Be the sweet presence of good diffused,
And in diffusion ever more intense!
So shall I join the choir invisible,
Whose music is the gladness of the world.

GEORGE ELIOT

W HAT THEN is the conclusion of the matter? Love yourself, if that means rational and healthy self-interest. You are commanded to do that. That is the length of life. Love your neighbor as you love yourself. You are commanded to do that. That is the breadth of life. But never forget that there is a first and even greater commandment: "Love the Lord thy God with all thy heart, and with all thy soul, and with all thy mind." This is the height of life. Only by a painstaking development of all three of these dimensions can you expect to live a complete life.

MARTIN LUTHER KING

INCLINE US, O God,
To think humbly of ourselves,
To be saved only in the examination of our own conduct,
To consider our fellow-creatures with kindness,
And to judge of all they say and do with the charity
Which we would desire from them ourselves.

JANE AUSTEN

S O FAR as in us lies, we must play the immortal and do all in
our power to live by the best element in our nature.

ARISTOTLE, *Nicomachean Ethics*

BE GENEROUS in prosperity, and thankful in adversity. Be worthy of the trust of thy neighbor, and look upon him with a bright and friendly face. Be a treasure to the poor, an admonisher to the rich, an answerer of the cry of the needy, a preserver of the sanctity of thy pledge. Be fair in thy judgment, and guarded in thy speech. Be unjust to no man, and show all meekness to all men. Be as a lamp unto them that walk in darkness, a joy to the sorrowful, a sea for the thirsty, a haven for the distressed, an upholder and defender of the victim of oppression. Let integrity and uprightness distinguish all thine acts. Be a home for the stranger, a balm to the suffering, a tower of strength for the fugitive. Be eyes to the blind, and a guiding light unto the feet of the erring. Be an ornament to the countenance of truth, a crown to the brow of fidelity, a pillar of the temple of righteousness, a breath of life to the body of mankind, an ensign of the hosts of justice, a luminary above the horizon of virtue, a dew to the soil of the human heart, an ark on the ocean of knowledge, a sun in the heaven of bounty, a gem on the diadem of wisdom, a shining light in the firmament of thy generation, a fruit upon the tree of humility.

BAHÁ'Í FAITH: *Gleanings 130*

# GOLDEN RULES FOR THE SOUL

Y OU SHALL love your neighbor as yourself.

JUDAISM: *Leviticus 19.18*

TSEKUNG ASKED, "Is there one word that can serve as a principle of conduct for life?" Confucius replied, "It is the word shu – reciprocity: Do not do to others what you do not want them to do to you."

CONFUCIANISM: Analects 15.23

HURT NOT others with that which pains yourself.

BUDDHISM: Udana 5.18

NOT ONE of you is a believer until he loves for his brother what he loves for himself.

ISLAM: Forty Hadith of an-Nawawi 13

D ESIRE NOT for anyone the things that ye would not desire for yourselves.

BAHÁ'Í FAITH: *Gleanings 66*

A LL THINGS whatsoever ye would that men should do to you, do ye even so to them: for this is the law and the prophets.

CHRISTIANITY: *Matthew 7.12*

N EVER DO to others what would pain thyself.

HINDUISM: *Pancatantra 3.104*

T REAT OTHERS as thou wouldst be treated thyself.

SIKHISM: *Adi Granth*

REGARD YOUR neighbor's gain as your own gain and your neighbor's loss as your own loss.

TAOISM: *T'ai Shang Kan Ying P'ien*

THAT NATURE only is good when it shall not do unto another whatever is not good for its own self.

ZOROASTRIANISM: *Dadistan-i-Dinik*

HE THAT does good to another does good also to himself, not only in the consequence but in the very act. For the consciousness of well-doing is in itself ample reward.

SENECA

WHAT THOU avoidest suffering thyself seek not to impose on others.

EPICTETUS, *Enchiridion*

GIVE TO every other human being every right that you claim yourself.

ROBERT G. INGERSOLL, *Limitations of Toleration*

THERE IS no other God than truth . . . To see the universal and all-pervading Spirit of Truth face to face one must be able to love the meanest of creation as oneself.

MOHANDAS K. GANDHI, *Autobiography*

# REALIZING YOUR SOUL'S POTENTIAL

*To be what we are, and to become what we are capable of becoming, is the only end of life.*

Robert Louis Stevenson,
*Familiar Studies of Men and Books*

# FREE WILL AND TRUE FREEDOM

EVERY HUMAN being has been given free will. If he wishes to incline himself toward the good way and to be righteous, he is free to do so; and if he wishes to incline himself toward the evil way and to be wicked he is free to do that . . . Every individual is capable of being righteous like Moses or wicked like Jeroboam, wise or foolish, merciful or cruel, mean or generous.

JUDAISM: *Mishneh Torah 5.1–3*

THE GREATEST gift that God in his bounty made in creation, and the most conformable to his goodness, and that which he prizes the most, was the freedom of will, with which the creatures with intelligence, they all and they alone, were and are endowed.

DANTE, *The Divine Comedy*

NO ONE says to a stone, "You are late," or to a
  stick, "Why did you strike that blow?"
Nor would you say such things to a person who
  has no free will, and only acts under
  compulsion.
Obligations and prohibitions, honor and rebuke
  only concern those who possess free will.
Human beings have free will in the matter of
  injustice and wrong-doing.
This free will is rooted in our inner spirit, in our
  hearts.

RUMI, *Masnavi V.2971–5*

GOD IS not willing to do everything, and thus take away our free will and that share of the glory that belongs to us.

NICCOLO MACHIAVELLI, *The Prince*

GOD NEVER draws anyone to himself by force and violence. He wishes all men to be saved, but forces no one.

ST. JOHN CHRYSOSTOM, *Sermon*

THERE ARE two freedoms – the false, where a man is free to do what he likes; and the true, where a man is free to do what he ought.

CHARLES KINGSLEY

WITHOUT COMMANDMENTS obliging us to live after a certain fashion, our existence is that of the "unemployed." This is the terrible spiritual situation in which the best youth of the world finds itself today. By dint of feeling itself free, exempt from restrictions, it feels itself empty.

JOSÉ ORTEGA Y GASSET, *Revolt of the Masses*

FREEDOM IS not procured by a full enjoyment of what is desired, but by controlling the desire.

EPICTETUS, *Discourses*

OUR WILLS are not ours to be crushed and broken; they are ours to be trained and strengthened.

HAMILTON WRIGHT MABIE, *The Life of the Spirit*

T HE WILL of God is the measure of things.

ST. AMBROSE

G IVE ME grace ever to desire and to will what is most acceptable to thee and most pleasing in thy sight.

THOMAS À KEMPIS, *The Imitation of Christ*

B E BOTH a servant and free: a servant in that you are subject to God, but free in that you are not enslaved to anything – either to empty praise or to any of the passions.

JOHN OF APAMEA

SOMETIMES WHEN I was a child my mother or father would say, "Shut your eyes and hold out your hand." That was the promise of some lovely surprise. I trusted them, so I shut my eyes instantly and held out my hand. Whatever they were going to give me I was ready to take. So it should be in our trust of our heavenly Father. Faith is the willingness to receive whatever he wants to give, or the willingness not to have what he does not want to give.

ELISABETH ELLIOT, *A Lamp for My Feet*

IF IT be Thy pleasure, make me to grow as a tender herb in the meadows of Thy grace, that the gentle winds of Thy will may stir me up and bend me into conformity with Thy pleasure in such wise that my movement and my stillness may be wholly directed by Thee.

BAHÁ'Í FAITH: *Prayers and Meditations 150*

TAKE MY life, and let it be
Consecrated Lord to Thee.
Take my moments and my days,
Let them flow in ceaseless praise.
Take my hands, and let them move
At the impulse of Thy love.
Take my feet and let them be
Swift and beautiful for Thee.

Take my voice, and let me sing
Always, only, for my King.
Take my lips, and let them be
Filled with messages from Thee.
Take my silver and my gold;
Not a mite would I withhold.
Take my intellect, and use
Every power as Thou shalt choose.

Take my will, and make it Thine;
It shall be no longer mine.
Take my heart, it is Thine own;
It shall be Thy royal throne.
Take my love, my Lord, I pour
At Thy feet its treasure store.
Take myself, and I will be
Ever, only, all for Thee.

FRANCES R. HAVERGAL

WHATEVER INSTRUMENT God makes of me, I become.
If He makes me a cup, I become a cup;
If He makes me a dagger, I become a dagger.
If He makes me a fountain, then I shall give water;
If He makes me fire, then I shall give heat.
If He makes me rain, I shall bring forth the harvest;
If He makes me an arrow, I shall pierce the body.
If He makes me a snake, I shall produce poison;
If He makes me His friend, I shall serve Him well.
I am like a pen in His hand which He moves as He
    wills.

RUMI, *Masnavi V.1685–90*

ETERNAL GOD,
The light of the minds that know you,
The life of the souls that love you,
The strength of the wills that serve you;
Help us so to know you that we may truly love you,
So to love you that we may fully serve you,
Whom to serve is perfect freedom.

POPE GELASIUS

N O MAN is a creature of will. According to what his will is in this world, so will he be when he has departed this life.

HINDUISM: *Chandogya Upanishad*

# DEVELOPING AN
# INTERNAL COMPASS

M Y DAD always used to say, "If you take a step and it feels good, you must be headed in the right direction." What he wanted us to understand was that we needed to measure our progress against our inner compass, using our feelings, our comfort level, and our knowledge of ourselves as the ultimate guide . . . I've spent most of my adult life trying to hear that inner voice above the noise around me.

LINDA WELTNER, *No Place Like Home*

ONSCIENCE IS a man's compass, and though the needle sometimes deviates, though one perceives irregularities in directing one's course by it, still one must try to follow its direction.

VINCENT VAN GOGH, *Dear Theo*

ONSCIENCE IS God's presence in man.

EMANUEL SWEDENBORG, *Heavenly Arcana*

HE TRUE guide of our conduct is no outward authority, but the voice of God, who comes down to dwell in our souls, who knows all our thoughts.

J.E.E. DALBERG-ACTON (LORD ACTON)

O GOD, THOU hast endowed conscience with no material force to compel man's reluctant obedience. So give them inwardly a spiritual compulsion in which they will follow it out of choice and delight.

M. KAMEL HUSSEIN, *City of Wrong*

I HAVE A certain divine sign from God . . . I have had it from childhood: it is a kind of voice which, whenever I hear it, always turns me back from something which I was going to do.

PLATO, *Apology*

T HE SUPREME end of education is expert discernment in all things – the power to tell the good from the bad, the genuine from the counterfeit, and to prefer the good and genuine to the bad and counterfeit.

SAMUEL JOHNSON

T HE GLORY of good men is in their conscience and not in the mouths of men.

THOMAS À KEMPIS, *The Imitation of Christ*

W HAT YOU think of yourself is far more important than what others think of you.

SENECA

WHEN A man is content with the testimony of his own conscience, he does not care to shine with the light of another's praise.

ST. BERNARD OF CLAIRVAUX, Letters

REAL GOODNESS does not attach itself merely to this life – it points to another world. Political or professional reputation cannot last forever, but a conscience void of offense before God and man is an inheritance for eternity.

DANIEL WEBSTER

REAL HUMAN progress depends upon a good conscience.

ALBERT EINSTEIN

# THE PATH OF SPIRITUAL
## DISCIPLINE

THE CENTRAL conception of man in the Gospels is that he is an unfinished creation capable of reaching a higher level by a definite evolution which must begin by his own efforts.

MAURICE NICOLL, *The New Man*

I T IS you who must make the effort. The Great of the past only show the Way.

BUDDHISM: *Dhammapada 276*

W HAT EXACTLY is the spiritual life? It is the life in which God and his eternal order have, more and more, their undivided sway; which is wholly turned to him, devoted to him, dependent on him, and which at its term and commonly at the price of a long and costly struggle, makes the human creature a pure capacity for God.

EVELYN UNDERHILL, *Mixed Pasture*

D EVELOPING THE muscles of the soul demands no competitive spirit, no killer instinct, although it may erect pain barriers that the spiritual athlete must crash through.

GERMAINE GREER

L IFE IS a succession of lessons which must be lived in order to be understood.

RALPH WALDO EMERSON

T HE SOUL must be trained . . . Withdraw into yourself and look. And if you do not find yourself beautiful as yet, do as does the sculptor of a statue that is to be made beautiful; he cuts away here, he smooths there, he makes this line lighter, this other purer, until he has shown a beautiful face upon his statue. So do you also; cut away all that is excessive, straighten all that is crooked, bring light to all that is shadowed, labor to make all glow with beauty, and do not cease chiseling your statue until there shall shine out on you the godlike splendor of virtue, until you shall see the final goodness surely established in the stainless shrine.

PLOTINUS, *The Enneads I.9*

H E IS best who is trained in the severest discipline.

KING ARCHIDAMUS OF SPARTA

B UDDHIST PRACTICE is a process of transformation through purification that brings out the best of what is already there. It does not make people into what they are not, nor import any new material. It allows your ultimate identity as an enlightened being to emerge as you overcome the relative delusions and defilements that mask your Buddha nature. It is transformation to your ultimate self.

THE TWELFTH TAI SITUPA, *Awakening the Sleeping Buddha*

D O NOT try to develop what is natural to man; develop what is natural to heaven. He who develops heaven benefits life; he who develops man injures life.

TAOISM: *Chuang Tzu 19*

THERE ALSO exists a sleeping sickness of the soul. Its most dangerous aspect is that one is unaware of its coming. That is why you have to be careful . . . You should realize your soul suffers if you live superficially.

ALBERT SCHWEITZER

A SPIRITUAL LIFE without discipline is impossible . . . The practice of a spiritual discipline makes us more sensitive to the small, gentle voice of God.

HENRI NOUWEN

WHAT YOU are must always displease you, if you would attain that which you are not.

ST. AUGUSTINE, *Sermons*

FAITH MEANS just that blessed unrest, deep and strong, which so urges the believer onward that he cannot settle at ease in the world and anyone who was quite at ease would cease to be a believer.

SØREN KIERKEGAARD, *Gospel of Suffering*

THERE IS nothing noble in being superior to some other man. The true nobility is in being superior to your previous self.

HINDUISM: A Proverb

THE LIGHT of a good character surpasseth the light of the sun and the radiance thereof. Whoso attaineth unto it is accounted as a jewel among men.

BAHÁ'Í FAITH: Tablets of Bahá'u'lláh 36

TRAIN YOURSELF in godliness; for while bodily training is of some value, godliness is of value in every way, as it holds promise for the present life and also for the life to come.

CHRISTIANITY: 1 Timothy 4.7–8

O MAN! VERILY you are ever toiling on toward your Lord – painfully toiling – but you shall meet Him . . . You shall surely travel from stage to stage.

ISLAM: Qur'an 84.6, 19

B Y DEGREES, little by little, from time to time, a wise person should remove his own impurities as a smith removes the dross from silver.

BUDDHISM: *Dhammapada 239*

O NE IMPORTANT direction in which to exercise gentleness is with respect to ourselves, never growing irritated with one's self or one's imperfections; for although it is but reasonable that we should be displeased and grieved at our own faults, yet ought we to guard against a bitter, angry, or peevish feeling about them . . . What we want is a quiet, steady, firm displeasure at our own faults . . . So then, when you have fallen, lift up your heart in quietness, humbling yourself deeply before God by reason of your frailty, without marveling that you fell; there is no cause to marvel because weakness is weak, or infirmity infirm. Heartily lament that you should have offended God, and begin anew to cultivate the lacking grace, with a very deep trust in His mercy, and with a bold, brave heart.

ST. FRANCIS DE SALES, *Introduction to the Devout Life*

# SELF-TRANSFORMATION

EVERYONE THINKS of changing humanity, and no one ever thinks of changing himself.

LEO TOLSTOY

T O BECOME spiritual, you must die to self, and come alive in the Lord. Only then will the mysteries of God fall from your lips. To die to self through self-discipline causes suffering but brings you everlasting life.

RUMI, Masnavi III.3364–5

L ET EACH one remember that he will make progress in all spiritual things only insofar as he rids himself of self-love, self-will, and self-interest.

ST. IGNATIUS LOYOLA, Spiritual Exercises

NO MAN can do properly what he is called upon to do in this life unless he can learn to forget his ego and act as an instrument of God.

W.H. AUDEN

GOOD ACTIONS and thoughts produce consequences which tend to neutralize, or put a stop to, the results of evil thoughts and actions. For as we give up the life of self (and note that, like forgiveness, repentance and humility are also special cases of giving), as we abandon what the German mystics called "the I, me, mine," we make ourselves progressively capable of receiving grace. By grace we are enabled to know reality more completely, and this knowledge of reality helps us to give up more of the life of selfhood – and so on, in a mounting spiral of illumination and regeneration.

ALDOUS HUXLEY, Huxley and God

THE COMPLETE mystic "way" includes both intellectual belief and practical activity; the latter consists in getting rid of the obstacles in the self and in stripping off its base characteristic and vicious morals, so that the heart may attain to freedom from what is not God and to constant recollection of Him.

AL-GHAZZALI, *Deliverance from Error*

FOR A man to conquer himself is the first and noblest of all victories.

PLATO

THEY ARE forever free who renounce all selfish desires and break away from the ego-cage of "I," "me," and "mine" to be united with the Lord. Attain to this, and pass from death to immortality.

HINDUISM: *Bhagavad Gita 2.71*

W HEN A man's fight begins within himself, he is worth something

ROBERT BROWNING

SEVER ME from myself that I may be grateful to you;
May I perish to myself that I may be safe in you;
May I die to myself that I may live in you;
May I wither to myself that I may blossom in you;
May I be emptied of myself that I may abound in you;
May I be nothing to myself that I may be all to you.

DESIDERIUS ERASMUS, *Abound in You*

O SON OF Man! If thou lovest Me, turn away from thyself; and if thou seekest My pleasure, regard not thine own; that thou mayest die in Me and I may eternally live in thee . . .

O My Servant! Free thyself from the fetters of this world, and loose thy soul from the prison of self. Seize thy chance, for it will come to thee no more.

BAHÁ'Í FAITH: *Arabic Hidden Words 7*
*Persian Hidden Words 40*

JESUS TOLD his disciples, "If any man would come after me, let him deny himself and take up his cross and follow me. For whoever would save his life will lose it, and whoever loses his life for my sake will find it."

CHRISTIANITY: *Matthew 16.24–5*

SELF IS the only prison that can ever bind the soul.

HENRY VAN DYKE, *The Prison and the Angel*

WHERE SELF exists, God is not;
Where God exists, there is no self.

SIKHISM: *Morning Prayer*

O GOD, HELP me to have victory over myself, for it is difficult to conquer oneself, though when that is conquered, all is conquered.

JAIN SCRIPTURES

LORD, ENFOLD me in the depths of your heart; and there hold me, refine, purge, and set me on fire, raise me aloft, until my own self knows utter annihilation.

PIERRE TEILHARD DE CHARDIN

L ORD, MAKE me according to thy heart.

BROTHER LAWRENCE,
*The Practice of the Presence of God*

T HE MASTER said, "At fifteen I set my heart upon learning. At thirty, I had planted my feet upon firm ground. At forty, I no longer suffered from perplexities. At fifty, I knew what were the biddings of heaven. At sixty, I heard them with a docile ear. At seventy, I could follow the dictates of my own heart; for what I desired no longer overstepped the boundaries of right."

CONFUCIANISM: *Analects 2.4*

V ERILY GOD does not reward man for what he does, but for what he is.

CHUANG-TZU

ONE MORNING a woman asked her lover, as a test, "Do you love me more than you love yourself?" He replied, "I love you so much that I am full of you from head to toe. There is nothing left of my own existence except my name." If you love God, you will feel toward Him as that lover felt toward his beloved.

RUMI, *Masnavi V.2020–4*

THE MASTER said, "Even when walking in a party of no more than three I can always be certain of learning from those I am with. There will be good qualities that I can select for imitation and bad ones that will teach me what requires correction in myself."

CONFUCIANISM: *Analects 7.21*

LET EACH morn be better than its eve and each morrow richer than its yesterday.

BAHÁ'Í FAITH: *Tablets of Bahá'u'lláh 138*

# PURIFYING THE HEART

B ETTER KEEP yourself clean and bright; you are the window through which you must see the world.

GEORGE BERNARD SHAW

B LESSED ARE the pure in heart, for they shall see God.

CHRISTIANITY: *Matthew* 5.8

T HE WHOLE point of this life is the healing of the heart's eye through which God is seen.

ST. AUGUSTINE OF HIPPO

I AM BLIND and do not see the things of this world; but when the light comes from above, it enlightens my heart and I can see, for the eye of my heart sees everything; and through this vision I can help my people. The heart is a sanctuary at the center of which there is a little space, wherein the Great Spirit dwells, and this is the eye. This is the eye of the Great Spirit by which he sees all things, and through which we see him. If the heart is not pure, the Great Spirit cannot be seen.

NATIVE AMERICAN TRADITION: *Black Elk*

EVERYONE SEES the inner reality of things, and even the future, according to her insight and spiritual enlightenment. This in turn increases in proportion to the purity of her heart. The more she polishes her heart's mirror, the more she can see in it, and the more the hidden mysteries are revealed to her. That spiritual purity is given to us by the grace of God, and our success in polishing our hearts is also a divine bounty.

RUMI, *Masnavi IV.2902, 2909–11*

THOU ART the life of the universe; to me
The light of day thou art, and the dark of night:
Activity's field when I do wake and see;
In sleep my dream. Oh, life of life, the light
Thou art to me of day, the dark of night.
Relieve me of my vice and virtue;
Make my heart void, and this heart made empty
Fill with thy entirety. Thy excelling take
And make me great with it. Enfold me still
Within thee: cover me, protector bright,
My light of day who art, and dark of night.

C.R. DAS

A PURE HEART is as a mirror; cleanse it with the burnish of love and severance from all save God, that the true sun may shine within it and the eternal morning dawn. Then wilt thou clearly see the meaning of, "Neither doth My earth nor My heaven contain Me, but the heart of my faithful servant containeth Me." And thou wilt take up thy life in thine hand, and with infinite longing cast it before the new Beloved One.

BAHÁ'Í FAITH: *The Seven Valleys 21–2*

THIS IS true religion; to cleanse oneself with pure thoughts, pure words, and pure deeds.

ZOROASTRIANISM: *Zend-Avesta*

IT IS only with the heart that one can see rightly; what is essential is invisible to the eye.

ANTOINE DE SAINT-EXUPÉRY

PURITY IS for man, next to life, the greatest good, that purity that is procured by the law of Mazda to him who cleanses his own self with good thoughts, words, and deeds.

ZOROASTRIANISM: *Zend-Avesta*

THE EYE is given sight through nearness to God.

RUMI, *Masnavi II.2309*

# A DAILY WORKOUT
# FOR THE SOUL

*What is a man,*
*If his chief good and market of his time*
*Be but to sleep and feed?*

SHAKESPEARE, *Hamlet IV.iv*

# PRAYER

**P**RAYER SHOULD be the key of the day and the lock of the night.

THOMAS FULLER, *Gnomologia*

IN THE life of the Indian there is only one inevitable duty – the duty of prayer – the daily recognition of the unseen and eternal.

NATIVE AMERICAN TRADITION: *Ohiyesa*

NO ONE should give the answer that it is impossible for a man occupied with worldly cares to pray always. You can set up an altar to God in your mind by means of prayer. And so it is fitting to pray at your trade, on a journey, standing at a counter, or sitting at your handicraft.

ST. JOHN CHRYSOSTOM

THERE IS not in the world a kind of life more sweet and delightful than that of a continual conversation with God.

BROTHER LAWRENCE,
*The Practice of the Presence of God*

BEFORE THE words of prayer come to the lips, the mind must believe in God's willingness to draw near to us, and in our ability to clear the path for his approach. Such belief is the idea that leads us toward prayer.

ABRAHAM JOSHUA HESCHEL,
*The Essence of Spiritual Living*

IT IS the language of the spirit which speaks to God. When, in prayer, we are freed from all outward things and turn to God, then it is as if in our hearts we hear the voice of God. Without words we speak, we communicate, we converse with God, and hear the answer . . . All of us, when we attain to a truly spiritual condition, can hear the Voice of God.

BAHÁ'Í FAITH: *Bahá'u'lláh and the New Era* 85–6

THE VALUE of persistent prayer is not that he will hear us . . . but that we will finally hear him.

WILLIAM McGILL

PRAYER IS exhaling the spirit of man and inhaling the spirit of God.

EDWIN KEITH

FOR ME, prayer is an upward leap of the heart, an untroubled glance toward heaven, a cry of gratitude and love, which I utter from the depths of sorrow as well as from the heights of joy. It has a supernatural grandeur that expands the soul and unites it with God.

ST. THÉRÈSE OF LISIEUX

IT DRAWS God who is great into a heart which is
small.
It drives the hungry soul up to the fullness of
God.

MECHTHILD OF MAGDEBURG

SEPARATION FROM God is like a well;
Remembrance of Him is the rope.

RUMI, *Divan-i Shams 19325*

PRAYER IS the service of the heart.

JUDAISM: *Talmud*

THERE IS a polish for everything that becomes rusty, and the polish for the heart is the remembrance of God.

ISLAM: *Hadith of Tirmidhi*

PRAYER IS the greatest of spells, the best healing of all remedies.

ZOROASTRIANISM: *The Yosht*

PRAYER TAKES the mind out of the narrowness of self-interest, and enables us to see the world in the mirror of the holy. For when we betake ourselves to the extreme opposite of the ego, we can behold a situation from the aspect of God. Prayer is a way to master what is inferior in us, to discern between the signal and the trivial, between the vital and the futile, by taking counsel with what we know about the will of God, by seeing our fate in proportion to God. Prayer clarifies our hopes and intentions. It helps us to discover our true aspirations, the pangs we ignore, the longings we forget. It is an act of self-purification, a quarantine for the soul.

Prayer implants in us the ideals we ought to cherish. Redemption, purity of mind and tongue, or willingness to help, may hover as ideas before our mind, but the idea becomes a concern, something to long for, a goal to be reached, when we pray . . . Prayer makes visible the right, and reveals what is hampering and false. In its radiance, we behold the worth of our efforts, the range of our hopes, and the meaning of our deeds.

ABRAHAM JOSHUA HESCHEL

W E ALL know pretty well why we come into retreat: we come to seek the opportunity of being alone with God and attending to God, in order that we may do his will better in our everyday lives. We have come to live for a few days the life of prayer and deepen our contact with the spiritual realities on which our lives depend – to recover if we can our spiritual poise.

EVELYN UNDERHILL, *The Fruits of the Spirit*

G IVE REST to the weary, visit the sick, support the poor; for this also is prayer.

AFRAHAT

T HE TIME of business does not differ from the time of prayer; and in the noise and clutter of my kitchen, while several persons are at the same time calling for different things, I possess God in as great tranquility as if I were on my knees at the blessed sacrament.

BROTHER LAWRENCE,
*The Practice of the Presence of God*

ALL EFFORT and exertion put forth by man from the fullness of his heart is worship, if it is prompted by the highest motives and the will to do service to humanity. This is worship: to serve mankind and to minister to the needs of the people. Service is prayer.

BAHÁ'Í FAITH: *Paris Talks 177*

VISIBLE WORSHIP is not condemned, but God is pleased only by invisible piety.

DESIDERIUS ERASMUS, *Enchiridion*

WHEN THOU prayest, rather let thy heart be without words than thy words be without heart.

JOHN BUNYAN

So the reality, the living quality of our prayer, our communion with God, can best be tested by the gradual growth in us of these fruits of divine love: love, joy, peace, long-sufferingness, gentleness, goodness, faithfulness, meekness, temperance – all the things the world most needs. A clear issue is it not? To discover the health and reality of our life of prayer, we need not analyze it or fuss about it. But we must consider whether it tends, or does not tend, to produce just these fruits, because they are the necessary results of the action of God in the soul. These are the fruits of human nature when it has opened itself to the action of the eternal love.

EVELYN UNDERHILL, *The Fruits of the Spirit*

# MEDITATION

I<small>T IS</small> of primary importance that a certain space of time be allotted daily to meditation on eternal things. No priest can omit this without a serious manifestation of negligence and without a grave loss to his soul.

P<small>OPE</small> P<small>IUS</small> X, Haerent animo

I HAVE FOUND that the door to meditation is open everywhere and at any time, at midnight, or at noonday, at dawn, or at dusk. Everywhere, on the street, on the trolley, on the train, in the waiting room, or in the prison cell, I am given a resting place of meditation, wherein I can meditate to my heart's content on the almighty God who abides in my heart.

TOYOHIKO KAGAWA

THOU ART divine, I know, O Lord supreme,
Since God found entrance to my heart through
   love.
This taught me that for steady inner growth
Quick and silent meditation's best.

ZOROASTRIANISM: *Zend-Avesta*

THAT HAPPINESS which belongs to a mind which by deep meditation has been washed clear of all impurity and has entered within the self, cannot be described by words; it can be felt by the inward power only.

HINDUISM: *Maitranyana Brahmana Upanishad*

THROUGH THE faculty of meditation man attains to eternal life; through it he receives the breath of the Holy Spirit – the bestowal of the Spirit is given in reflection and meditation. The spirit of man is itself informed and strengthened during meditation; through it affairs of which man knew nothing are unfolded before his view.

BAHÁ'Í FAITH: *Paris Talks 175*

SUFIS ARE a mirror for the soul – better than a
   mirror,
For they have polished their hearts in
   remembrance of God and meditation,
Until their heart's mirror reflects a true image of
   the Original.

RUMI, *Masnavi I.3153–4*


A BLESSED BOOK have We sent down to thee, that men may
meditate its verses, and that those endued with
understanding may bear it in mind.

ISLAM: *Qur'an 38.29*

WHEN MEDITATION is mastered, the mind is unwavering like the flame of a lamp in a windless place. In the still mind, in the depths of meditation, the eternal self reveals itself. Beholding the self by means of the self, an aspirant knows the joy and peace of complete fulfillment. Having attained that abiding joy beyond the senses, revealed in the stilled mind, he never swerves from the central truth. He desires nothing else, and cannot be shaken by the heaviest burden of sorrow. The practice of meditation frees one from all affliction. This is the path of yoga . . .

Wherever the mind wanders, restless and diffuse in its search for satisfaction without, lead it within; train it to rest in the self. Abiding joy comes to those who still the mind. Freeing themselves from the taint of self-will, with their consciousness unified, they become one with God.

HINDUISM: *Bhagavad Gita 6.18–27*

THIS BOOK of the law shall not depart out of thy mouth, but thou shalt meditate therein day and night, that thou mayest observe to do according to all that is written therein; for then thou shalt make thy ways prosperous, and then thou shalt have good success. Have not I commanded thee? Be strong and of good courage; be not affrighted, neither be thou dismayed: for the Lord thy God is with thee withersoever thou goest.

JUDAISM: *Joshua 1.8–9*

MEDITATION IS no other thing than the attentive thought, voluntarily reiterated and entertained in the mind, to excite the will to holy and salutary affections and resolutions.

ST. FRANCIS DE SALES, *Treatise on the Love of God*

IT IS meditation that leads us in spirit to the hallowed solitudes wherein we find God alone – in peace, in calm, in silence, in recollection.

J. CRASSET, *A Key to Meditation*

WITHOUT KNOWLEDGE there is no meditation, without meditation there is no knowledge. He who has knowledge and meditation is near to Nirvana.

BUDDHISM: *Dhammapada 372*

THERE IS a story regarding the Buddha that recounts how he once gave teaching to a famous sitar player who wanted to study meditation. The musician asked, "Should I control my mind, or should I completely let it go?" The Buddha answered, "Since you are a great musician, tell me how you would tune the strings of your instrument." The musician said, "I would make them not too tight, and not too loose." "Likewise," said the Buddha, "in your meditation practice you should not impose anything too forcefully on your mind, nor should you let it wander." That is the teaching of letting the mind be in a very open way, of feeling the flow of energy without trying to subdue it and without letting it get out of control, or going with the energy pattern of mind. This is meditation practice.

CHÖGYAM TRUNGPA

BETTER THAN a hundred years lived in ignorance, without contemplation, is one single day of life lived in wisdom and in deep contemplation.

BUDDHISM: *Dhammapada 111*

# GOOD DEEDS AND
## LITTLE KINDNESSES

G OD CREATED the physical universe in order to manifest
Himself, so that the treasure of His wisdom may be
revealed. He said, "I was a hidden treasure." Listen! In
the same way you must not let your spiritual reality be
submerged, but instead must manifest your spirit in action.

RUMI, *Masnavi IV.3028–9*

ABU HURAIRA reported God's Messenger as saying, "God does not look at your forms and your possessions, but He looks at your hearts and your deeds."

ISLAM: *Hadith of Muslim*

BE YE doers of the word, and not hearers only. For as the body without the spirit is dead, so faith without works is dead also.

CHRISTIANITY: *James 1.22*

AS A flower that is lovely and beautiful, but is scentless, even so fruitless is the well-spoken word of one who does not practice it.

BUDDHISM: *Dhammapada 51*

I N THIS world, aspirants may find enlightenment by two different paths. For the contemplative is the path of knowledge; for the active is the path of selfless action.

HINDUISM: Bhagavad Gita 3.3

W HEN YOU leave this world, material riches will be left behind; but every good that you have done will go with you.

Life should be chiefly service. Without that ideal, the intelligence that God has given you is not reaching out toward its goal. When in service you forget the little self, you will feel the big Self of Spirit.

PARAMAHANSA YOGANANDA

ONE DAY a man asked a sheikh how to reach God. "The ways to God," the sheikh replied, "are as many as there are created beings. But the shortest and easiest is to serve others, not to harm others, and to make others happy."

ABU SA'ID

MY COUNTRY is the world, and my religion is to do good.

THOMAS PAINE, *The Rights of Man*

I EXPECT TO pass through this world but once. Any good therefore that I can do, or any kindness or abilities that I can show to any fellow creature, let me do it now. Let me not defer or neglect it, for I shall not pass this way again.

WILLIAM PENN

THE HEART benevolent and kind
The most resembles God.

ROBERT BURNS, *A Winter Night*

THAT BEST portion of a good man's life,
His little, nameless, unremembered acts
Of kindness and of love.

WILLIAM WORDSWORTH,
*Lines Composed above Tintern Abbey*

ALL THE kindness which a man puts out into the world works on the heart and thoughts of mankind.

ALBERT SCHWEITZER,
*Memoirs of Childhood and Youth*

TO BRING joy to a single heart is better than to build many shrines for worship.

ABU SA'ID

A MAN OF humanity is one who, in seeking to establish himself, finds a foothold for others and who, desiring attainment for himself, helps others to attain.

CONFUCIANISM: *Analects*

LET NO one ever come to you without leaving better and happier. Be the living expression of God's kindness; kindness in your face, kindness in your eyes, kindness in your smile, kindness in your warm greeting.

MOTHER TERESA

THE ESSENCE of all religions is love, compassion, and tolerance. Kindness is my true religion. No matter whether you are learned or not, whether you believe in the next life or not, whether you believe in God or Buddha or some other religion or not, in day-to-day life you must be a kind person . . . Love, compassion, and tolerance are necessities, not luxuries. Without them, humanity cannot survive. If you have a particular faith or religion, that is good. But you can survive without it if you have love, compassion, and tolerance. The clear proof of a person's love of God is if that person genuinely shows love to fellow human beings.

THE DALAI LAMA, *Love, Compassion, and Tolerance*

SIMPLY BE the mirror in which others can see themselves as God sees them.

EDWARD HAYS, *The Gospel of Gabriel*

TREAT PEOPLE as if they were what they ought to be and you help them to become what they are capable of being.

J.W. VON GOETHE

IT IS no great thing to get on well with good and docile men, for that is naturally pleasant to all people, and all men gladly have peace with those and most love those who are agreeable. But to live peacefully with evil men and with impertinent men who lack good manners and are illiterate and rub us the wrong way – that is a great grace, and manly deed, and much to be praised, for it cannot be done save through great spiritual strength.

THOMAS À KEMPIS, *The Imitation of Christ*

GOD HAS been very gracious to me, for I never dwell upon anything wrong which a person has done, so as to remember it afterwards. If I do remember it, I always see some other virtue in that person.

ST. TERESA OF ÁVILA

TO BE silent concerning the faults of others, to pray for them, and to help them, through kindness, to correct their faults.

To look always at the good and not at the bad. If a man has ten good qualities and one bad one, to look at the ten and forget the one; and if a man has ten bad qualities and one good one, to look at the one and forget the ten.

Never to allow ourselves to speak one unkind word about another, even though that other be our enemy.

BAHÁ'Í FAITH: *Bahá'u'lláh and the New Era 80*

WE HAVE no more right to consume happiness without producing it than to consume wealth without producing it.

GEORGE BERNARD SHAW

WE MAKE a living by what we get, we make a life by what we give.

SIR WINSTON CHURCHILL

# BEAUTIFYING THE SOUL

MAN IS like a precious stone: cut and polished by morals, adorned by wisdom.

ISAAC F. SATANOV, *Mishle Asaf*

VIRTUE IS a kind of health, beauty, and habit of the soul.

PLATO, *The Republic*

VIRTUES AND graces are the signs of a follower of
   God;
They are the footprints of one who is devoted to
   Him.

RUMI, *Masnavi II.1665*

BIRTH DOES not lead to greatness; but the cultivation of virtues by a person leads him to greatness.

JAINISM: *Vajjalagam 687*

F OLLOW AND worship God in the exercise of virtue, for this way of worshiping God is the most holy.

FLAVIUS JOSEPHUS, *Against Apion*

T HEY ASKED a Chinese wise man, "What is science?" He said, "Science is to know people." Then they asked, "And what is virtue?" He answered, "Virtue is to love people."

LEO TOLSTOY, *A Calendar of Wisdom*

N O BEAUTY leaves such an impression, strikes so deep, or links the souls of men closer than virtue.

ROBERT BURTON, *Anatomy of Melancholy*

SWEETER THAN the perfume of sandalwood or of the lotus-flower is the perfume of virtue.

BUDDHISM: *Dhammapada 55*

GOD CREATED humankind so that humankind might cultivate the earthly and thereby create the heavenly.

HILDEGARD OF BINGEN, *Illuminations*

MAN MUST acquire heavenly qualities and attain divine attributes. He must become the image and likeness of God. He must seek the bounty of the eternal, become the manifester of the love of God, the light of guidance, the tree of life, and the depository of the bounties of God. That is to say, man must sacrifice the qualities and attributes of the world of nature for the qualities and attributes of the world of God.

BAHÁ'Í FAITH: *Promulgation of Universal Peace 451*

THE FRUITS of the spirit are those dispositions, those ways of thinking, speaking, and acting, which are brought forth in us, gradually but inevitably, by the pressure of divine love in our souls. They all spring from that one root. We might call them manifestations of the mind of God in his creation.

EVELYN UNDERHILL, *The Fruits of the Spirit*

SPIRITUALITY I take to be concerned with those qualities of the human spirit – such as love and compassion, a sense of responsibility, a sense of harmony – which bring happiness to both self and others. Whilst ritual and prayer, along with the questions of nirvana and salvation, are directly connected with religious faith, these inner qualities need not be, however. Thus there is no reason why the individual should not develop them, even to a high degree, without recourse to any religious or metaphysical belief system. This is why I sometimes say that religion is something we can perhaps do without. What we cannot do without are these basic spiritual qualities.

THE DALAI LAMA, *Ancient Wisdom, Modern World*

I HAVE never seen in this world of trial and probation
Anything more highly prized than a good character.
Whoever has a good temperament and character
    is saved on the Day of Judgment,
While those who are not pure-hearted and virtuous
    are broken.

RUMI, *Masnavi II.810, 816*

ABU HURAIRA reported God's Messenger as saying, "The believers whose faith is most perfect are those who have the best character."

ISLAM: *Hadith of Abu Dawud and Darimi*

WASTE NO time arguing what a good man should be: be one.

MARCUS AURELIUS

# A DAILY CHECK-UP

**T**HE UNEXAMINED life is not worth living.

SOCRATES

I SHALL TELL you a great secret, my friend. Do not wait for the last judgment. It takes place every day.

ALBERT CAMUS

O NLY OUR concept of time makes it possible for us to speak of the day of judgment by that name; in reality it is a summary court in perpetual session.

FRANZ KAFKA

T RULY AT the day of judgment we shall not be examined on what we have read, but what we have done; not how well we have spoken, but how religiously we have lived.

THOMAS À KEMPIS, *The Imitation of Christ*

H UMAN BEINGS judge one another by their external actions. God judges them by their moral choices.

C.S. LEWIS, *Christian Behavior*

I F, WHEN you look into your own heart, you find nothing wrong there, what is there to worry about, what is there to fear?

CONFUCIUS

T O PRAY means to accept and to remember the laws of the limitless being, God, and to measure all your deeds in the past and in the future according to his laws. And it is useful to do this as often as possible.

LEO TOLSTOY, *A Calendar of Wisdom*

E ACH OF you should examine his own conduct, and then he can measure his achievement by comparing himself to himself and not with anyone else; for everyone has his own burden to bear.

CHRISTIANITY: *Galatians 6.4–5*

S ET BEFORE thine eyes God's unerring Balance and, as one standing in His Presence, weigh in that Balance thine actions every day, every moment of thy life. Bring thyself to account ere thou art summoned to a reckoning.

BAHÁ'Í FAITH: *Gleanings 235*

A WAKE, YE sleepers from your sleep . . . and ponder over your deeds; remember your creator and go back to him in penitence. Be not of those who miss realities in their pursuit of shadows and waste their years in seeking after vain things which cannot profit or deliver. Look well to your souls and consider your acts; forsake each of you his wrong ways and improper thoughts and return to God so that he may have mercy on you.

MOSES MAIMONIDES

IF YOU sit down at set of sun
And count the acts that you have done,
  And, counting, find
One self-denying deed, one word
That eased the heart of him who heard,
  One glance most kind
That fell like sunshine where it went –
Then you may count that day well spent.

But if, through all the livelong day,
You've cheered no heart, by yea or nay –
  If, through it all
You've nothing done that you can trace
That brought the sunshine to one face –
  No act most small
That helped some soul and nothing cost –
Then count that day as worse than lost.

GEORGE ELIOT

# HEALING YOUR SOUL

*The man who regards his own life and that of his fellow creatures as meaningless is not merely unfortunate but almost disqualified for life.*

ALBERT EINSTEIN, *The World As I See It*

# OVERCOMING THE NEGATIVE

B E PATIENT with everyone, but above all with yourself. I mean, do not be disheartened by your imperfections, but always rise up with fresh courage.

ST. FRANCIS DE SALES

THE NAME of God may be written upon that soul thou treadest on.

SAMUEL TAYLOR COLERIDGE, *Aids to Reflection*

GOD HIMSELF, Sir, does not propose to judge a man until the end of his days.

SAMUEL JOHNSON

WE FEEL and weigh soon enough what we suffer from others, but how much others suffer from us, of this we take no heed.

THOMAS À KEMPIS, *The Imitation of Christ*

I AM THE entire human race compacted together. I have found that there is no ingredient of the race which I do not possess in either a small way or a large way.

MARK TWAIN

WHOEVER SEES all beings in himself and himself in all beings does not, by virtue of such realization, hate anyone.

HINDUISM: *Isa Upanishads*

LIFE APPEARS to me to be too short to be spent in nursing animosity or in registering wrongs. We are, and must be, one and all, burdened with faults in this world; but the time will come when, I trust, we shall put them off in putting off our corruptible bodies; when debasement and sin will fall from us and only the spark will remain . . . With this creed, revenge never worries my heart, degradation never too deeply disgusts me, injustice never crushes me too low. I live in calm, looking to the end.

CHARLOTTE BRONTË

CONQUER ANGER by love. Conquer evil by good. Conquer the mean by generosity. Conquer the liar by truth . . . Never in the world is hatred conquered by hatred: hatred is conquered by love.

BUDDHISM: *Dhammapada 223, 5*

FORGIVING MEANS to pardon the unpardonable and loving means to love the unlovable. Or it is no virtue at all.

G.K. CHESTERTON

A MAN THAT studieth revenge keeps his own wounds green, which otherwise would heal and do well.

FRANCIS BACON

L OVE IS the only force capable of transforming an enemy into a friend.

MARTIN LUTHER KING

I F WE could read the secret history of our enemies, we would find in each man's life a sorrow and a suffering enough to disarm all hostility.

HENRY WADSWORTH LONGFELLOW

T HOSE WHO are at war with others are not at peace with themselves.

WILLIAM HAZLITT

A PERSISTENT TRAP all along the path is pride in one's spiritual purity.

RAM DAS

THE LIAR'S punishment is not in the least that he is not believed, but that he cannot believe anyone else.

GEORGE BERNARD SHAW

IT IS the preoccupation with possession, more than anything else, that prevents man from living freely and nobly.

BERTRAND RUSSELL

DO NOT care overly much for wealth or power or fame, or one day you will meet someone who cares for none of these things, and you will realize how poor you have become.

RUDYARD KIPLING

LET NOT your mind run on what you lack as much as on what you have already. Of the things you have, select the best; and then reflect how eagerly they would have been sought if you did not have them.

MARCUS AURELIUS

ENJOY YOUR life without comparing it with that of others.

MARQUIS DE CONDORCET

NEARLY ALL men can stand adversity, but if you want to test a man's character, give him power.

ABRAHAM LINCOLN

B ETTER TO stumble with the toe than with the tongue.

SWAHILI PROVERB

T HE TONGUE is a small thing, but what enormous damage it can do. A great forest can be set on fire by one tiny spark. And the tongue is a flame of fire. It is full of wickedness and poisons every part of the body. And the tongue is set on fire by hell itself, and can turn our whole lives into a blazing flame of destruction and disaster.

CHRISTIANITY: *James 3.2–6*

# TESTS AND DIFFICULTIES

H UMAN BEINGS are like untanned hide: apply bitter acids and rub them in vigorously and the leather will become soft and supple and full of beauty. Similarly, if you tan the human soul with harsh discipline and suffering, it will gradually become pure, lovely, and very strong. But if you cannot mortify yourself, accept the sufferings God sends you, for afflictions sent by the Friend are the means of your purification. The medicine becomes palatable to the sick when they focus on their health.

RUMI, *Masnavi IV.104–8*

O MY LORD, how certain it is that anyone who renders you some service soon pays with a great trial! And what a precious reward a trial is for those who truly love you if we could at once understand its value!

St. Teresa of Ávila

T HE MORE the diamond is cut, the brighter it sparkles; and what seems hard dealing, there God has no end in view but to perfect his people.

Thomas Guthrie

W ERE IT not for tests, pure gold could not be distinguished from the impure. Were it not for tests, the courageous could not be separated from the cowardly. Were it not for tests, the people of faithfulness could not be known from the disloyal . . . Were it not for tests, sparkling gems could not be known from worthless pebbles.

Bahá'í Faith: *The Divine Art of Living*

THE GEM cannot be polished without friction, nor man perfected without trials.

CONFUCIUS

THE SHELL must break before the bird can fly.

ALFRED, LORD TENNYSON

IN THE Buddhist tradition, difficulties are considered to be so important to a life of growth and peace that a Tibetan prayer actually asks for them . . . It is felt that when life is too easy, there are fewer opportunities for genuine growth.

RICHARD CARLSON

GOLF WITHOUT bunkers and hazards would be tame and monotonous. So would life.

B.C. FORBES

MANY MEN owe the grandeur of their lives to their tremendous difficulties.

CHARLES H. SPURGEON

I THANK GOD for my handicaps, for, through them, I have found myself, my work, and my God.

HELEN KELLER

THE POWERS of the soul are commensurate with its needs.

RALPH WALDO EMERSON

THE BEAUTY of the soul shines out when a man bears with composure one heavy mischance after another, not because he does not feel them, but because he is a man of high and heroic temper.

ARISTOTLE, *Nicomachean Ethics*

IF THERE be anywhere on earth a lover of God who is always kept safe from falling, I know nothing of it – for it was not shown me. But this was shown – that in falling and rising again we are always held close in one love.

JULIAN OF NORWICH, *Revelations of Divine Love*

WHATEVER HAPPENS, abide steadfast in a determination to cling simply to God.

ST. FRANCIS DE SALES

Perseverance is a great element of success. If you only knock long enough and loud enough at the gate, you are sure to wake up somebody.

HENRY WADSWORTH LONGFELLOW

# GRIEF AND SUFFERING

CHARACTER CANNOT be developed in ease and quiet. Only through experience of trial and suffering can the soul be strengthened, vision cleared, ambition inspired, and success achieved.

HELEN KELLER

THERE IS no coming to consciousness without pain.

CARL JUNG

A DEEP DISTRESS hath humanized my soul.

WILLIAM WORDSWORTH

TRULY ONE learns only by sorrow; it is a terrible education that the soul gets and it requires a terrible grief that shakes the very foundation of one's being to bring the soul into its own.

MAJOR LANOE HAWKER, V.C.

BESTOW, O GOD, this grace upon us, that in the school of suffering we should learn self-conquest, and through sorrow, even if it be against our will, learn self-control.

AESCHYLUS

GRIEF AND sorrow do not come to us by chance; they are sent to us by the divine mercy for our own perfecting . . . Men who suffer not, attain no perfection. The plant most pruned by the gardeners is that one which, when the summer comes, will have the most beautiful blossoms and the most abundant fruit.

BAHÁ'Í FAITH: *Paris Talks 50*

WHEN HEAVEN is about to confer a great office on any man, it first exercises his mind with suffering, and his sinews and bones with toil.

MENG-TZE, *The Book of Meng-Tze*

WHEN SUFFERINGS come upon him man must utter thanks to God, for suffering draws man near unto the holy one, blessed be he.

RABBI ELEAZAR BEN JACOB

PAIN MAKES men think,
Thinking gives man wisdom:
And wisdom confers peace.

BORIS PASTERNAK

THE WORD "happiness" would lose its meaning if it were not balanced by sadness.

CARL JUNG

IF ALL our misfortunes were laid in one common heap whence everyone must take an equal portion, most people would be contented to take their own and depart.

SOCRATES

MAN IS fond of counting his troubles, but he does not count his joys. If he counted them up as he ought to, he would see that every lot has enough happiness provided for it.

FYODOR DOSTOEVSKY

EARTH HAS no sorrow that heaven cannot heal.

SIR THOMAS MORE, *Come, Ye Disconsolate*

THERE IS no grief which time does not lessen and soften.

CICERO

ALTHOUGH THE world is full of suffering, it is also full of the overcoming of it.

HELEN KELLER

TIMES BRING changes.

UGANDAN PROVERB

MAKE YOURSELVES nests of pleasant thoughts. None of us yet know, for none of us have been taught in early youth, what fairy palaces we may build of beautiful thoughts – proof against all adversity. Bright fancies, satisfied memories, noble histories, faithful sayings, treasure-houses of precious and restful thoughts, which care cannot disturb, nor pain make gloomy, nor poverty take away from us – houses built without hands, for our souls to live in.

JOHN RUSKIN

HAVE COURAGE for the great sorrows of life and patience for the small ones; and when you have laboriously accomplished your daily task, go to sleep in peace. God is awake.

VICTOR HUGO

# PEACE AND HAPPINESS

PEACE COMES within the souls of men when they realize their relationship, their oneness, with the universe and all its powers, and when they realize that at the center of the Universe dwells Wakan Tanka, and that this center is really everywhere, it is within each of us.

NATIVE AMERICAN TRADITION: *Black Elk*

THOU DOST keep him in perfect peace,
Whose mind is stayed on Thee.

JUDAISM: *Isaiah 26.3*

FOR THE man who forsakes all desires and abandons all pride of possession and of self reaches the goal of peace supreme.

HINDUISM: *Bhagavad Gita 2.71*

DISCIPLINE, TO be sure, is never pleasant; at times it seems painful, but afterwards those who have been trained by it reap the harvest of a peaceful and upright life.

CHRISTIANITY: *Hebrews 12.11*

IBELIEVE THE root of all happiness on this earth to lie in the
realization of a spiritual life with a consciousness of
something wider than materialism; in the capacity to live in
a world that makes you unselfish because you are not
overanxious about your personal place; that makes you
tolerant because you realize your own comic fallibilities; that
gives you tranquility without complacency because you believe
in something so much larger than yourself.

SIR HUGH WALPOLE

HAPPINESS IS, literally, God within, or good.

MARCUS AURELIUS, *Meditations*

SINCE HAPPINESS is nothing else but the enjoyment of the
supreme good, and the supreme good is above us, no one
can be happy who does not rise above himself.

ST. BONAVENTURE, *The Journey of the Mind to God*

INWARDNESS, MILDNESS, and self-renouncement do make for man's happiness.

MATTHEW ARNOLD

A MAN'S FELICITY consists not in the outward and visible blessings of fortune, but in the inward and unseen perfections and riches of the mind.

ANACHARSIS

WHAT A man *is* contributes much more to his happiness than what he *has* . . . What a man is in himself, what accompanies him when he is alone, what no one can give him or take away, is obviously more essential to him than everything he has in the way of possessions, or even what he may be in the eyes of the world.

ARTHUR SCHOPENHAUER

T HE SUPREME happiness of life is the conviction that we are loved.

VICTOR HUGO, *Les Misérables*

O NE OF the things I keep learning is that the secret of being happy is doing things for other people.

DICK GREGORY

I T IS only well with me when I have a chisel in my hand.

MICHELANGELO

TRUE HAPPINESS flows from the possession of wisdom and virtue and not from the possession of external goods.

ARISTOTLE, *Politics*

MONEY MAY buy the husk of things, but not the kernel. It brings you food but not appetite, medicine but not health, acquaintances but not friends, servants but not faithfulness, days of joy but not peace or happiness.

HENRIK IBSEN

I HAVE NOTICED that folks are generally about as happy as they make up their minds to be.

ABRAHAM LINCOLN

GRANT ME, O Lord, the royalty of inward happiness and the serenity which comes from living close to thee. Daily renew the sense of joy, and let the eternal spirit of the Father dwell in my soul and body, filling every corner of my heart with light and grace, so that bearing about with me the infection of a good courage, I may be a diffuser of life and may meet all ills and crosses with gallant and high-hearted happiness, giving thee thanks always for all things.

ROBERT LOUIS STEVENSON

*Peace and Happiness* 189

GOD GRANT me the serenity to accept the things
that cannot be changed; courage to change
the things I can; and wisdom to know the
difference.
Living one day at a time;
Enjoying one moment at a time;
Accepting hardships as the pathway to peace;
Taking this sinful world as it is, not as I would
have it;
Trusting that you will make all things right if I
surrender to your will;
That I may be reasonably happy in this life
And supremely happy with you forever in the
next.

REINHOLD NIEBUHR, *The Serenity Prayer*

# THE JOURNEY'S END

*Science has found that nothing can disappear without a trace. Nature does not know extinction. All it knows is transformation.*

WERNHER VON BRAUN

# THE IMMORTALITY
## OF THE SOUL

SURELY GOD would not have created such a being as man, with an ability to grasp the infinite, to exist only for a day! No, man was made for immortality.

ABRAHAM LINCOLN

I F I ERR in my belief that the souls of men are immortal, I err gladly, and I do not wish to lose so delightful an error.

CICERO, *De Senectute*

S HALL WE believe that the soul, which is invisible, and which goes hence to a place that is like herself, glorious, and pure, and invisible, to hades, which is rightly called the unseen world to dwell with the good and wise God (whither, if it be the will of God, my soul too must shortly go) – shall we believe that the soul, whose nature is so glorious, and pure, and invisible, is blown away by the winds and perishes as soon as she leaves the body, as the world says?

SOCRATES, *The Phaedo*

I TROUBLE NOT myself about the manner of future existence. I content myself with believing, even to positive conviction, that the power that gave me existence is able to continue it, in any form and manner he pleases, either with or without this body; and it appears more probable to me that I shall continue to exist hereafter than that I should have had existence, as I now have, before that existence began.

THOMAS PAINE, *The Age of Reason*

I T IS not born, nor does it ever die, nor having come to be will it ever more come not to be. Unborn, eternal, everlasting, this ancient one [soul] is not slain when the body is slain.

HINDUISM: *Bhagavad Gita 2.20*

T HE BODY dies but the spirit is not entombed.

BUDDHISM: *Dhammapada 151*

ALL THE living must die, and dying, return to the ground; this is what is called *kuei*. The bones and flesh molder below, and, hidden away, become the earth of the fields. But the spirit issues forth, and is displayed on high in a condition of glorious brightness.

CONFUCIANISM: *Book of Ritual 21.2.1*

THOU ART My light and My light shall never be extinguished, why dost thou dread extinction? Thou art My glory and My glory fadeth not; thou art My robe and My robe shall never be outworn. Abide then in thy love for Me, that thou mayest find Me in the realm of glory.

BAHÁ'Í FAITH: *Arabic Hidden Words 14*

WOE IS he . . . who has gathered riches and counted them over, thinking his riches have made him immortal!

ISLAM: *Qur'an 104.1–3*

NEITHER EXPERIENCE nor science has given man the idea of immortality . . . The idea of immortality rises from the very depths of his soul – he feels, he sees, he knows that he is immortal.

FRANÇOIS GUIZOT

HE WHO attains Tao is everlasting. Though his body may decay he never perishes.

TAOISM: Tao Te Ching

# DEATH AND TRANSFORMATION

T HAT DAY which you fear as being the end of all things is
the birthday of your eternity.

SENECA, *Letters to Lucilius*

D EATH IS the supreme festival on the road to freedom.

DIETRICH BONHOEFFER, *Letters from Prison*

T HOUGH THOU sleepest, thou wakest again; though thou diest, thou livest again.

INSCRIPTION ON ROYAL EGYPTIAN TOMB

THERE IS no death! What seems so is transition;
This life of mortal breath
Is but a suburb of the life elysian,
Whose portal we call death.

HENRY WADSWORTH LONGFELLOW, *Resignation*

T HERE IS no death. Only a change of worlds.

NATIVE AMERICAN TRADITION: *Chief Seattle*

W HAT THE caterpillar calls a tragedy, the Master calls a butterfly.

RICHARD BACH

L IFE IS a great surprise; I do not see why death should not be a greater one.

VLADIMIR NABOKOV

D EATH IS in reality spiritual birth, the release of the spirit from the prison of the senses into the freedom of God, just as physical birth is the release of the baby from the prison of the womb into the freedom of the world. While childbirth causes pain and suffering to the mother, for the baby it brings liberation.

RUMI, *Masnavi III.3556–60*

B ARTER NOT the garden of eternal delight for the dust-heap of a mortal world. Up from thy prison ascend unto the glorious meads above, and from thy mortal cage wing thy flight unto the paradise of the Placeless.

BAHÁ'Í FAITH: *Persian Hidden Words 39*

WHEN YOU take the wires of the cage apart, you do not hurt the bird, but you help it. You let it out of its prison. How do you know that death does not help me when it takes the wires of my cage down? – that it does not release me, and put me into some better place and better condition of life?

BISHOP RANDOLPH S. FOSTER

AS A man passes from dream to wakefulness, so does he pass from this life to the next.

HINDUISM: *Brihadaranyaka Upanishad 4.3.35*

YANZI SAID: "How well the men of old understood death! The good find rest in it, the wicked submit to it." Dying is the virtue in us going to its destination. The men of old called a dead man "a man who has gone back." Saying that the dead have gone back they implied that the living are travelers. The traveler who forgets to go back is a man who mistakes his home.

TAOISM: *Liezi 1, Heaven's Gifts*

ONE WHO identifies himself with his soul regards the transmigration of his soul at death fearlessly, like changing one cloth for another.

JAINISM: *Pujyapada, Samadhishataka 77*

O SON OF the Supreme! I have made death a messenger of joy to thee. Wherefore dost thou grieve?

BAHÁ'Í FAITH: *Arabic Hidden Words 32*

IN THE Buddhist approach, life and death are seen as one whole, where death is the beginning of another chapter of life. Death is a mirror in which the entire meaning of life is reflected.

SOGYAL RINPOCHE

WHAT IS this world? A dream within a dream – as we grow older each step is an awakening. The grave the last sleep? – no: it is the last and final awakening.

WALTER SCOTT, *Journal*

WHAT IS our death but a night's sleep? For as through sleep all weariness and faintness pass away and cease, and the powers of the spirit come back again, so that in the morning we arise fresh, and strong, and joyous; so at the last day we shall rise again as if we had only slept a night, and shall be fresh and strong.

MARTIN LUTHER

VITAL SPARK of heavenly flame!
Quit, O quit this mortal frame!
Trembling, hoping, lingering, flying,
O the pain, the bliss of dying!
Cease, fond nature, cease thy strife,
And let me languish into life!

Hark! they whisper; angels say,
'Sister spirit, come away!'
What is this absorbs me quite?
Steals my senses, shuts my sight,
Drowns my spirits, draws my breath?
Tell me, my soul, can this be death?

The world recedes; it disappears!
Heaven opens on my eyes, my ears
With sounds seraphic ring.
Lend, lend your wings! I mount! I fly!
O grave! where is thy victory?
O death! where is thy sting!

ALEXANDER POPE

# THE WORLD BEYOND

THE HUMBLE, meek, merciful, just, pious, and devout souls are everywhere of one religion; and when death has taken off the mask they will know one another, though the divers liveries they wear here make them strangers.

WILLIAM PENN, *Friends and the Christian Church*

THE DIFFERENCE between the old Narnia and the new Narnia was like that. The new one was a deeper country: every rock and flower and blade of grass looked as if it meant more. I can't describe it any better than that: if you ever get there you will know what I mean.

It was the Unicorn who summed up what everyone was feeling. He stamped his right fore-hoof on the ground and neighed and then cried: "I have come home at last! This is my real country! I belong here. This is the land I have been looking for all my life, though I never knew it till now. The reason why we loved the old Narnia is that it sometimes looked a little like this . . . Come farther up and farther in!"

C.S. Lewis

D O NOT grudge your brother his rest. He has at last become free, safe, and immortal, and ranges joyous through the boundless heavens; he has left this low-lying region and has soared upward to that place which receives in its happy bosom the souls set free from the chains of matter.

Your brother has not lost the light of day, but has obtained a more enduring light. He has not left us, but has gone on before.

SENECA

N OT LIKE this world is the world to come. In the world to come there is neither eating nor drinking; no procreation of children or business transactions; no envy or hatred or rivalry; but the righteous sit enthroned, their crowns on their heads, and enjoy the luster of the divine splendor.

JUDAISM: *Talmud*

WHEN THE human soul soareth out of this transient heap of dust and riseth into the world of God, then veils will fall away, and verities will come to light, and all things unknown before will be made clear, and hidden truths be understood.

BAHÁ'Í FAITH: *Selections from the Writings of 'Abdu'l Bahá*

RELATIVES AND friends and well-wishers rejoice at the arrival of a man who had been long absent and has returned home safely from afar. Likewise, meritorious deeds will receive the good person upon his arrival in the next world, as relatives welcome a dear one on his return.

BUDDHISM: *Dhammapada 219–20*

NAUGHT IS the life of the world save a pastime and a sport. Better far is the abode of the Hereafter for those who keep their duty to God. Have ye then no sense?

ISLAM: *Qur'an 6.32*

HE IS happy in this world and he is happy in the next world: the man who does good is happy in both worlds. He is glad, he feels great gladness when he sees the good he has done.

BUDDHISM: *Dhammapada 16*

THEN AS for him whose scales are heavy with
   good works,
He will live a pleasant life.
But as for him whose scales are light,
A bereft and Hungry One will be his mother,
Ah, what will convey unto thee what she is! –
Raging Fire.

ISLAM: Qur'an 101.6–11

BRING US, O Lord, at our last awakening to the house and
gate of heaven, to enter into that gate and dwell in that
house where there shall be no darkness nor dazzling but
one equal light, no noise nor silence but one equal music.

JOHN DONNE

# THE SOUL'S HOMECOMING

L IFE IS a voyage that's homeward bound.

HERMAN MELVILLE

WHAT BETTER can the Lord do for a man than take him home when he has done his work?

CHARLES KINGSLEY

NEVER SAY about anything, "I have lost it," but only "I have given it back." Is your child dead? It has been given back. Is your wife dead? She has been returned.

EPICTETUS

DEATH IS a bridge between friends. The time now nears that I cross that bridge, and friend meets Friend.

RÁBI'A

MY LORD, it is time to move on.
Well, then, may your will be done.
O my Lord and my spouse,
The hour that I have longed for has come.
It is time for us to meet one another.

ST. TERESA OF ÁVILA

GOING TO heaven!
I don't know when,
Pray do not ask me how –
Indeed I'm too astonished
To think of answering you!
Going to heaven!
How dim it sounds!
And yet it will be done
As sure as flocks go home at
    night
Unto the shepherd's arm!

Perhaps you're going too!
Who knows?
If you should get there first
Save just a little space for me
Close to the two I lost –
The smallest "robe" will fit me
And just a bit of "crown" –
For you know we do not mind our dress
When we are going home.

EMILY DICKINSON

THE SUPREME desire of everything, and that first given by nature, is to return to its source; and since God is the source of our souls and maker of them . . . to him this soul desires above all to return.

DANTE, *The Banquet*

THE DUST returns to the earth as it was, and the spirit returns to God who gave it.

JUDAISM: *Ecclesiastes 12.7*

THOSE WHO remember me at the time of death will come to me. Do not doubt this. Whatever occupies the mind at the time of death determines the destiny of the dying; always they will tend toward that state of being. Therefore, remember me at all times.

HINDUISM: *Bhagavad Gita 8.5–7*

THE WEALTH of the other world is nearness to God.

BAHÁ'Í FAITH: *Some Answered Questions 231*

O LORD, MAY the end of my life be the best of it; may my closing acts be my best acts, and may the best of my days be the day when I shall meet Thee.

ISLAM

GOD GAVE you life and bestowed on you His attributes; eventually you will return to Him.

RUMI, *Masnavi III.4182*

WHEN HE thus departs, life departs; and when life departs, all the functions of the vital principle depart. The self remains conscious, and, conscious, the dying man goes to his abode. The deeds of this life, and the impressions they leave behind, follow him . . .

As a goldsmith, taking an old gold ornament, molds it to another, newer and more beautiful, so the self, having given up the body and left it unconscious, takes on a newer and better form.

HINDUISM: *Brihadaranyaka Upanishad 4.4.1–4*

KNOW THOU of a truth that the soul, after its separation from the body, will continue to progress until it attaineth the presence of God, in a state and condition which neither the revolution of ages and centuries, nor the changes and chances of this world, can alter . . .

The world beyond is as different from this world as this world is different from that of the child while still in the womb of its mother. When the soul attains the Presence of God, it will assume the form that best befits its immortality and is worthy of its celestial habitation.

BAHÁ'Í FAITH: *Gleanings 79, 157*

THE WORLD is like a courtroom, with God as our judge. We are called upon to fulfill our covenant with God, who asked, "Am I not your Lord?" To which we answered, "Yea." And since here on earth we are on trial, our every word and action form the witnesses to and the evidence of that agreement.

RUMI, *Masnavi V.174–6*

TOWARD THE wicked man and the righteous one
And him in whom right and wrong meet
Shall the Judge act in upright manner,
According to the laws of the present existence.

ZOROASTRIANISM: *Avesta, Yasna 33.1*

THEN I saw a great white throne and him who sat upon it; from his presence earth and sky fled away, and no place was found for them. And I saw the dead, great and small, standing before the throne, and the books were opened. Also another book was opened, which is the book of life. And the dead were judged by what was written in the books, by what they had done.

CHRISTIANITY: *Revelation 20.11–12*

KNOW ALSO that everything is according to reckoning; and let not your imagination give you hope that the grave will be a place of refuge for you. For perforce you were formed, and perforce you were born, and perforce you live, and perforce you will die, and perforce you will in the future have to give account and reckoning before the King of kings, the holy one, blessed be he.

JUDAISM: *Mishnah, Abot 4.29*

AND EVERY man's augury have We fastened to his own neck, and We shall bring forth from him on the Day of Resurrection a book which he will find wide open. "Read your book! Your soul suffices as a reckoner against you this day."

ISLAM: *Qur'an 17.13–14*

# ACKNOWLEDGEMENTS

*Every effort has been made to trace and acknowledge ownership of copyright. If any required credits have been omitted or any rights overlooked, it is completely unintentional. The publishers will be glad to make suitable arrangements with any copyright holder whom it has not been possible to contact, and would like to acknowledge the following for permission to reproduce material in this book.*

W.H. Auden by permission of Edward Mendelson • *What Personal Life?* © 1997 Rev. Michael Beckwith, by permission of New World Library • Dietrich Bonhoeffer, selection from *Letters and Papers from Prison, the Enlarged Edition*, SCM Press 1971 • Albert Camus by permission of Jean and Catherine Camus • G.K. Chesterton by permission of A. P. Watt • Winston Churchill by permission of Curtis Brown Group Limited • The Dalai Lama from *Love, Compassion, and Tolerance*, 1990 by permission of New World Library • The Dalai Lama from *Ancient Wisdom, Modern World*, 1999 by permission of Little, Brown • Chandra Devanesen from *Morning, Noon & Night* edited by the Reverend John Carden. Used by permission of the Church Mission Society • Albert Einstein from *The World as I See it*, 1934 by permission of Albert Einstein Archives • *The Long Journey Home* © 1990 Riane Eisler, by permission of New World Library • Elisabeth Elliot from *A Lamp for my Feet*, 1987 by permission of Servant Publications • Germaine Greer by permission of Gillon Aitken Associates Ltd • Dag Hammarskjöld from *Markings*, 1964 by permission of Faber & Faber Ltd and Alfred A. Knopf Inc. • Edward Hays from *The Gospel of Gabriel*, 1996 by permission of Forest of Peace Publishing, Inc • Aldous Huxley from *Huxley and God: Essays Edited by Jacqueline Bridgeman* © 1992 Jacqueline Bridgeman, by permission of Harper Collins Inc. • Aldous Huxley from *The Perennial Philosophy*, 1945 by permission of The Reece

Halsey Agency • Daniel Jordan from *Becoming Your True Self*, 1999 by permission of the Bahá'í Publishing Trust • Carl Jung by permission of Niedieck Linder AG • *Peace of Mind* © 1946 Joshua Loth Liebman, by permission of Simon and Schuster • Martin Luther King by permission of Intellectual Properties Management • C.S. Lewis from *Christian Behaviour*, 1943 and *The Last Battle*, 1956 by permission of Curtis Brown Group Limited • Thomas Merton by permission of Anne H. McCormick • Thomas Moore from *Care of the Soul*, 1992 by permission of Piatkus Books • Mother Teresa by permission of Servant Publications • Vladimir Nabokov by permission of Peter L. Skolnik • *Being Peace* © 1987 Thich Nhat Hanh, by permission of Parallax Press • José Ortega y Gasset from *Revolt of the Masses*, 1930 by permission of W.W. Norton & Company • Bertrand Russell by permission of the Bertrand Russell Archives Copyright Permissions Committee • Albert Schweitzer from *Memoirs of Childhood and Youth*, 1931 by permission of Macmillan Publishers Ltd • The Society of Authors is the literary representative of the estate of George Bernard Shaw • Teilhard de Chardin from Le Milieu Divin • A.J. Toynbee from *An Historian's Approach to Religion*, 1956 by permission of Oxford University Press • Chögyam Trungpa from *Cutting through Spiritual Materialism*, 1973 by permission of Shambhala Publications • The Twelfth Tai Situpa from *Awakening the Sleeping Buddha*, 1996 by permission of Shambhala Publications • Henry Van Dyke from *The Prison and the Angel* by permission of Ariel Press • Linda Weltner from *No Place Like Home*, 1988 by permission of William Morrow & Co. Inc. • Paramahansa Yogananda from Self Realization Summer 1983 (Los Angeles: Self-Realization Fellowship, 1983)•

# INDEX OF AUTHORS AND SOURCES